Weeknight
WONDERS

ASHLEY CRAFT

**52 Weeks of Fun, Themed Recipes the
Whole Family Can Make Together**

ROCK
POINT

First published in 2025 by Rock Point,
an imprint of The Quarto Group,
142 West 36th Street, 4th Floor,
New York, NY 10018, USA
(212) 779-4972
www.Quarto.com

EEA Representation, WTS Tax d.o.o.,
žanova ulica 3, 4000 Kranj, Slovenia.
www.wts-tax.si

Rock Point titles are also available at discount for retail, wholesale, promotional and bulk purchase. For details, contact the Special Sales Manager by email at specialsales@quarto.com or by mail at The Quarto Group, Attn: Special Sales Manager, 100 Cummings Center Suite, 265D, Beverly, MA 01915, USA.

10 9 8 7 6 5 4 3 2 1

ISBN: 978-1-57715-522-5

Digital edition published in 2025
eISBN: 978-0-7603-9580-6
Library of Congress Cataloging-in-Publication Data

Names: Craft, Ashley, author.
Title: Weeknight wonders : 52 weeks of fun themed recipes the whole family can make together / Ashley Craft.
Description: New York, NY, USA : Rock Point, 2025. |
Includes index. | Summary: "Make lasting family memories with the Weeknight Wonders cookbook, featuring 52 weeks of holiday- and culture-themed recipes that even the littlest chefs can accomplish"-- Provided by publisher.
Identifiers: LCCN 2025003443 (print) | LCCN 2025003444 (ebook) | ISBN 9781577155225 | ISBN 9780760395806 (ebook)
Subjects: LCSH: International cooking. | Holiday cooking. | LCGFT: Cookbooks.
Classification: LCC TX725.A1 C6393 2025 (print) | LCC TX725.A1 (ebook) | DDC 641.5/68--dc23/eng/20250208
LC record available at https://lccn.loc.gov/2025003443
LC ebook record available at https://lccn.loc.gov/2025003444

Publisher: Rage Kindelsperger
Creative Director: Laura Drew
Photo Art Director: Marisa Kwek
Editorial Director: Erin Canning
Managing Editor: Cara Donaldson
Project Editor: Melissa Haskin
Cover Design: Maeve Bargman and Marisa Kwek
Interior Design and Illustration: Maeve Bargman
Photography and Food Styling: Lorena Masso

Printed in Huizhou, Guangdong, China TT062025

To Elliot, Hazel, and Clifford—
the original members of
"The Cool Kids Cooking Club."

Contents

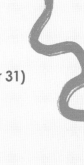

Introduction

Hi there! I'm Ashley Craft, the author of this book. As a wife, mother of three, and cookbook author, I have firsthand experience with the challenges of picky eating. Over the years, we've experimented with various strategies to broaden our children's palates and improve their nutritional intake.

One approach that proved incredibly effective was involving our kids in the cooking process. From grocery shopping to prepping ingredients and stirring pots, their participation significantly increased their willingness to try new foods. When they took ownership of a meal, they developed a sense of pride and accomplishment, making them more likely to taste what they helped create.

Whether you're facing picky eaters or simply want to strengthen family bonds, this book is designed to make mealtime a shared experience. Busy schedules often limit a family's time for elaborate cooking projects, which is why I've included only 3 recipes per week. It's hard to try something new, so I encourage you to mix and match these recipes with weeknight meals you already know. There's no shame in ordering a pizza, either!

In my house, we find that Saturdays are the best day for family cooking. Everyone is home and we have all day, so we stack our work and usually knock out 2 or 3 recipes in one day and then eat leftovers over the next few days. This may work for you or you may prefer to spread the cooking out over the week. Do whatever works best for your family! These moments, when you and your family work together in the kitchen, can create lasting memories and foster a love for food.

I hope you enjoy this cookbook and share your culinary creations with me on Instagram @UnofficialTasteTester!

How to Use
THIS BOOK

Included in this book are 52 themed weeks, with 3 recipes per week. Each recipe includes instructions for where and how to get your kids involved. As you make your way through these recipes, consider:

- The 52 themed weeks are placed in "order" to align with certain holidays throughout the year; however, you do not have to follow them in order! No one week builds on another, they are each separate.

- These recipes have tips to include different members of the family in the preparation process: Little Helping Hands (3+), Big Kids in the Kitchen (7+), Tweens on the Scene (11+), and Budding Sous-Chefs (17+). They are meant for the whole family to enjoy, including you! Parents can only eat so many chicken nuggets. I've done my best to make these recipes accessible to everyone in the family.

- Each recipe has a footnote with a tip for a certain-age child to help with one aspect of the recipe. You do not have to limit your children's involvement to that one step, or limit your children based on that age group. Read each recipe in advance and consider your own children and how they can best help prepare the dish. YOU know your children best and know what they can and cannot do!

The most important thing is to have fun! This book is meant to bring families together, not break them apart—so if any part of the book is not serving your family, skip it and move to another section! How you use the book is completely up to you.

Kitchen Tools

Here I have recommended equipment that will not only make your food preparation easier but also safer in some cases. If you don't have these items on hand, you can still easily cook the recipes found throughout this book.

BOX CHOPPER

This handy kitchen tool is a plastic box with a hinged lid equipped with various attachment blades resembling a crosshatch pattern. Simply place the item you want to chop on the blades, slam down the hinged lid, and watch as it dices the entire item in one swift motion. While it is significantly safer than using a knife, you should always ensure your fingers are clear before closing the lid.

BREAD MACHINE

This versatile appliance simplifies the bread-making process by mixing, kneading, rising, and baking bread in one convenient device. Compared to traditional hand kneading and oven baking, using a bread machine is significantly easier. You can often find used bread machines at thrift stores for a budget-friendly option.

COOKIE SCOOP

This tool isn't just for portioning cookie dough. Cookie scoops are ideal for scooping a variety of ingredients like muffin and pancake batter, ice cream, and more. Keep three sizes on hand—small, medium, and large—to accommodate your various scooping needs.

CUT-RESISTANT GLOVES

Online retailers offer adult- and child-size cut-resistant gloves made from materials that are highly resistant to knife penetration such as tightly woven polyethylene fibers. While young children should never use knives unsupervised, these gloves can provide added safety as you teach older children proper knife-handling techniques.

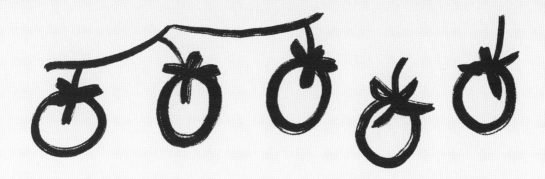

DISPOSABLE GLOVES

Kitchen safety extends beyond just preventing cuts. Harmful bacteria can reside on food and surfaces if not properly cleaned. To help contain the spread of bacteria, have family members wear disposable latex or rubber gloves when handling raw meat in the kitchen. Remember to replace your gloves each time you step away from the meat to prevent contamination.

FOOD PROCESSOR

A food processor is a specialized blender designed for chopping dry ingredients. It offers more consistent chopping and mixing results, making tasks like preparing piecrusts or sauces a breeze. Have an adult install the sharp blades, and then younger family members can safely operate the food processor.

GRAPE/CHERRY TOMATO CUTTER

This convenient tool efficiently quarters grapes and cherry tomatoes with a quick press. As grapes and cherry tomatoes can pose a choking hazard for young children, cutting them into smaller pieces is essential. While not strictly necessary, this tool simplifies the process of preparing these fruits.

HOT DOG COOKER

An optional kitchen appliance, the hot dog cooker steams hot dogs in a user-friendly tray. Simply add water, turn on the dial, and remove the hot dogs when cooked. If you have children who enjoy making hot dogs, a hot dog cooker can provide them with a sense of independence. However, hot dogs can be prepared just as easily in the microwave, making the hot dog cooker a purely optional addition to your kitchen.

INFRARED THERMOMETER GUN

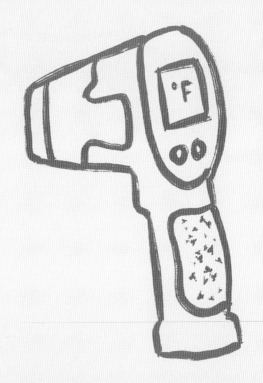

A kitchen thermometer is crucial for verifying the doneness of food and the temperature of mixtures. These devices are generally easier for children to use compared to traditional candy mercury thermometers because all you have to do is point it at the food you would like to check and press a button.

MICROWAVEABLE PASTA COOKER

While not strictly necessary as you likely have other suitable tools, the microwaveable pasta cooker offers convenience and ease of use, especially for children. This plastic container with perforated holes in the lid simplifies the pasta-making process. Simply add pasta and water as directed and microwave for the recommended time. Your children can independently start the process but assist them when it is time to remove the hot container from the microwave and drain the scalding water.

RICE COOKER

A rice cooker is a specialized kitchen appliance designed exclusively for making rice. Simply wash the rice, add it to the inner pot, pour in the recommended amount of water, and press the start button. While cooking rice on the stovetop is also a viable option, a rice maker offers greater ease of use for children as it eliminates the need for open flames or hot pan exteriors.

ROLLING PIN WITH THICKNESS RINGS

Rolling pins come in various styles, but one particularly helpful feature for children is thickness rings. These attachments slide onto each end of the rolling pin, determining the thickness of the dough when rolled out. The rings are usually labeled with their corresponding thickness and can be purchased online.

ROTARY CHEESE AND VEGETABLE GRATER

This essential kitchen tool features a suction cup base to secure it to the countertop, a circular grating surface, and a crank. Simply place the cheese or vegetable in the top chamber, press down on the guard, and crank the handle. Enjoy perfectly grated cheese or shredded vegetables without the risk of injuring your fingers.

SAFETY KNIVES

For families with young children, safety knives are essential kitchen tools. These plastic knives offer a safer alternative to traditional metal knives while still providing effective cutting capabilities. A serrated edge ensures efficient cutting performance. You can find sets of safety knives at online retailers.

SQUEEZE BOTTLE CONDIMENTS

Many grocery stores now offer condiments in squeeze bottles instead of jars. These bottles are more child friendly, as squeezing is easier (and more fun) than opening a jar and using a spoon. This allows children to participate more actively in kitchen tasks.

NEW YEAR WEEK

(JANUARY 1)

Happy New Year! New Year's Eve is on December 31, and New Year's Day is on January 1, ushering in a brand-new year. It can be a time of reflection of the old year and looking forward to what you can accomplish in the new year. Staying up until midnight on New Year's Eve is totally optional but is a fun way to "see" the new year begin. Here's how to make New Year Week fun in your home:

- Write down some resolutions or goals that you'd like to work on in the new year. You can make family goals and individual goals. The key is to make achievable benchmarks, so you don't get discouraged if your goal isn't realized immediately. Post them someplace the whole family can see them and encourage one another!

- Want to try something new? In Spain, for each chime of the clock at midnight, everyone tries to eat one grape. If you're doing the math, that's 12 grapes eaten in 12 seconds! You can adapt this challenge with grapes cut in halves or fourths so everyone can participate.

- In some places, personal fireworks are not legal, but there are "firework adjacent" options you can look for at the store, like party poppers, sparklers, or even just confetti. Find a way to make the celebration fun!

BLACK-EYED PEA SOUP

SERVES 6

1 tablespoon olive oil

1 medium yellow onion, diced

2 teaspoons minced garlic

1 can (15 ounces, or 425 g) black-eyed peas, rinsed and drained

8 cups (2 L) chicken broth

1 smoked ham hock (1 pound, or 454 g)

1 bay leaf

1 tablespoon ground cumin

1 tablespoon garlic powder

1 tablespoon salt

1 teaspoon dried thyme

1 teaspoon dried oregano

1 teaspoon smoked paprika

½ teaspoon ground black pepper

1 cup (150 g) cubed cooked ham

Sour cream, for garnishing

NOTE

BLACK-EYED PEAS ARE EATEN ON JANUARY 1 IN MANY SOUTHERN HOMES FOR GOOD LUCK THROUGH THE YEAR.

1. In a large pot over medium heat, heat the olive oil. Once shimmering, add the onion and cook until soft, about 5 minutes. Stir in the garlic and cook for 1 minute more.

2. Add the black-eyed peas, chicken broth, ham hock, bay leaf, cumin, garlic powder, salt, thyme, oregano, paprika, and pepper. Stir and bring to a boil over medium-high heat. Reduce the heat to low, cover, and let simmer for 1 hour, stirring occasionally. Add the cubed ham and cook for 10 minutes more.

3. Remove the pot from the heat. Discard the bay leaf. Transfer the ham hock to a cutting board and pull off as much meat as possible. Return the meat to the soup and discard the bones. Stir everything together.

4. Ladle into bowls and top with a dollop of sour cream and serve.

5. Leftovers can be stored in an airtight container in the refrigerator for up to 5 days.

LITTLE HELPING HANDS (3+)

Place each seasoning in its own small bowl. While you work on step 1, have your little ones smell each spice. Then, invite them to add each spice to the pot.

FIREWORK SUNDAES

MAKES 4 SUNDAES

8 scoops vanilla ice cream

1 packet (0.37 ounces, or 10.5 g)
Pop Rocks

Optional Toppings

Whipped cream

Peanuts

Sprinkles

Chocolate sauce

Caramel sauce

Mini chocolate chips

Maraschino cherries

1. Divide 8 scoops of ice cream evenly among 4 bowls. Top with your desired toppings.

2. Sprinkle each with Pop Rocks. The candy will start popping right away so serve immediately.

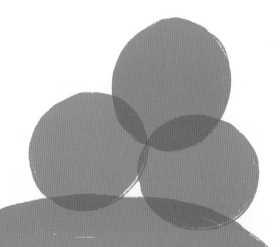

TWEENS ON THE SCENE (11+)

Scooping ice cream can take some muscle, so be sure to let your tween know their strength is needed! Warm up an ice cream scoop by holding it under hot tap water for 30 seconds to make the job a bit easier.

FIZZY BERRY DELIGHT

MAKES 4 DELIGHTS

1 cup (165 g) sliced fresh strawberries

½ cup (60 g) fresh raspberries

2 ounces (60 ml) fresh lime juice

2 ounces (60 ml) simple

Ice

1 bottle (25.4 ounces, or 750 ml) sparkling cider

1. In a cocktail shaker, add the strawberries, raspberries, lime juice, and simple syrup. Muddle and mash the mixture for 1 minute. Add 1 scoop of ice, secure the lid, and shake for 30 seconds.

2. Pour the sparkling cider into fluted glasses and strain the berry mixture into the cider. Stir gently and serve immediately.

LITTLE HELPING HANDS (3+)

Muddling is the act of mashing up ingredients in a cocktail shaker. Bartenders use a special tool called a muddler for this but if you don't have one, try using a small whisk instead. Even the littlest of kitchen helpers can mush and mash, so get them working on this drink!

TIP

TO MAKE THIS DRINK FOR A **PARTY**, SIMPLY MULTIPLY THE INGREDIENTS TIMES THE NUMBER OF GUESTS YOU HAVE (SEE IF YOUR TWEEN CAN DO THE MATH!) AND ADD A FEW EXTRA SERVINGS. THEN, **MUDDLE** THE **FRUIT** IN A **LARGE PUNCH BOWL** OR PITCHER, ADD ICE, POUR IN THE CIDER, **STIR**, AND **ENJOY!**

UKRAINE WEEK

(DAY OF UKRAINIAN UNITY, JANUARY 22)

January 22 marks Ukrainian Unity Day (or Den' Sobornosti), which is the day in 1919 when East and West Ukraine came together as one state. The holiday is usually marked with flags, parades, and concerts.

Depending on the region, temperatures are typically well below freezing in January. Thus, this holiday is typically filled with hearty and soul-warming dishes, such as:

- **KOMPOT.** Kompot is a refreshing, fruit-based drink. Fruits or dried fruits like pears and sour cherries are boiled in water, then the fruit is removed. It is served hot or cold.

- **CHICKEN NOODLE SOUP.** What is better to eat on a cold winter's day than chicken noodle soup? It is comforting and easy to whip together. Sometimes Ukrainians will add dumplings or dill to their soup for extra texture and flavor.

- **SWEET VARENIKI.** Vareniki are like little personal pie packets! Ukrainians use many different fruits in the filling, as well as different toppings to make their vareniki just so. Other options for toppings include melted butter and sour cream. When I'm in a sweets mood, I like to top my vareniki with chocolate syrup and sprinkles.

KOMPOT

SERVES 6

⅓ cup (45 g) dried apricots
⅓ cup (30 g) dried apples
⅓ cup (50 g) dried cherries
½ cup (120 ml) honey
1 cinnamon stick

NOTE

IF YOU WOULD LIKE TO SERVE THE KOMPOT CHILLED, PLACE THE FILLED PITCHER OR MUGS IN THE REFRIGERATOR UNTIL COOLED, ABOUT 1 HOUR. ADD SOME ICE IF YOU'D LIKE.

1. In a large pot over medium heat, stir together 4 cups (960 ml) of water and the apricots, apples, cherries, honey, and cinnamon stick. Bring to a boil over medium-high heat. Reduce the heat to low and let simmer for 20 minutes. Remove the pot from the heat and let the mixture cool for 10 minutes.

2. Carefully pour the mixture through a strainer into a pitcher or directly into heat-resistant mugs (see Note) and serve immediately.

LITTLE HELPING HANDS (3+)

To allow your little ones to help out, have them add all of the ingredients to a cold pot while it is on the counter or tabletop, then transfer the pot to the stove once it is filled. This allows them to feel included and keeps them away from hot liquids.

CHICKEN NOODLE SOUP

SERVES 6

2 tablespoons salted butter

1 medium yellow onion, diced

1 large carrot, peeled and diced

2 ribs celery, diced

2 tablespoons chopped fresh flat-leaf parsley, plus more for garnishing

4 cups (960 ml) chicken broth

½ teaspoon dried thyme

1 teaspoon salt

½ teaspoon ground black pepper

2 cups (75 g) wide egg noodles

1 cup (195 g) shredded cooked chicken

1. In a large pot over medium heat, melt the butter. Cook for about 2 minutes, or until bubbles form. Add the onion, carrot, and celery and cook, stirring occasionally, for 5 to 7 minutes, until the vegetables are soft. Stir in the parsley and cook 1 minute more.

2. Pour in the chicken broth, stir, and then add the thyme, salt, and pepper. Bring to a boil.

3. Add the egg noodles and reduce the heat to medium-low. Cook, stirring frequently, for 10 to 12 minutes, until the noodles are al dente. Add the chicken, stir, and cook until warmed through, about 2 minutes.

4. Sprinkle with parsley and serve.

BUDDING SOUS-CHEFS (17+)

Chopping vegetables can be finicky and even dangerous, especially round ones like carrots that might roll around. Start with a safety knife and have an adult cut the carrots in half lengthwise. Then the carrot can sit more firmly on its flat side on the cutting board and your teen can chop the rest of the carrots.

SWEET VARENIKI

MAKES 12 VARENIKI

Dough

2 cups (250 g) all-purpose flour, plus more for dusting

1 large egg

2 tablespoons vegetable oil

½ teaspoon salt

½ cup (120 ml) warm water

Filling

⅓ cup (80 g) peeled and diced Granny Smith apples

⅓ cup (50 g) frozen cherries

⅓ cup (50 g) frozen blueberries

6 tablespoons granulated sugar, divided

3 teaspoons cornstarch, divided

3 teaspoons fresh lemon juice, divided

½ cup (65 g) confectioners' sugar

LITTLE HELPING HANDS (3+)

Measuring frozen fruit is a breeze, and anyone can do it! Allow your little ones to scoop the measuring cup right into the bag of frozen fruit.

1. To make the dough: In a large bowl, beat the flour, egg, vegetable oil, salt, and warm water on low until a shaggy dough forms. Turn off the mixer, cover the bowl with a clean kitchen towel, and let the mixture rest for 5 minutes.

2. Uncover and switch to a dough hook. Knead on low for 5 to 7 minutes more, until the dough becomes smooth and elastic. Use your hands to shape the dough into a large ball. Return the ball to the bowl, cover with plastic wrap, and allow to rest for 30 minutes.

3. Meanwhile, prepare the filling: Place the apples in a medium bowl, the cherries in another, and the blueberries in a third bowl. To each bowl, add 2 tablespoons of the sugar, 1 teaspoon of the cornstarch, and 1 teaspoon of the lemon juice. Stir the contents of each bowl, separately, until the fruits are evenly coated.

4. Bring a large pot of water to a boil over high heat.

5. Lightly flour a large clean work surface. Use a lightly floured rolling pin to roll out the dough to ⅛-inch (3 mm) thickness. Use a round biscuit cutter (or just the rim of a glass) to cut out circles of dough that are about 3 inches (8 cm) in diameter.

6. Run a wet finger around the outer ¼ inch (6 mm) of a dough circle. Scoop 1 to 2 teaspoons of the apple mixture, the cherry mixture, or the blueberry mixture into the center of a dough circle and fold in half to seal. Pinch closed. Repeat until all the filling has been used. You should have about 12 vareniki.

7. Working in batches of about 6 at a time, carefully drop the vareniki into the boiling water and cook for 3 to 4 minutes, until they float to the surface. Use a slotted spoon to transfer the vareniki to a paper towel–lined plate.

8. Dust with confectioners' sugar before serving.

CHINA WEEK

(LUNAR NEW YEAR)

Most Americans celebrate the New Year on January 1, but in the Chinese lunar calendar, the New Year can land anywhere between January 21 and February 20. No matter what day you plan to celebrate, here are some ways to ring in the Chinese New Year:

- **SPRING CLEAN.** Sweep away the bad luck of the old year and start fresh.

- **DECORATE WITH THE COLOR RED.** In China, red is considered a lucky color. Because of this, many Chinese New Year decorations are red. In fact, children and elders often receive little red envelopes full of cash. How can you incorporate some red into your house this week?

- **HOST A GATHERING OR FESTIVAL.** Fireworks were invented in China and are still an integral part of Lunar New Year celebrations. Families are also likely to gather together for meals and parties. Consider hosting your own gathering. Eating noodles, wontons, and rice dishes will also help bring in luck, and I've included a recipe for each in this section. Noodles signify a long life, wontons symbolize purses of money, and rice represents abundance in all things. Happy Chinese New Year!

VEGGIE FRIED RICE

SERVES 6

2 tablespoons vegetable oil, divided

2 large eggs, beaten

1 cup (135 g) frozen mixed vegetables

3 cups (600 g) cooked rice (see Tip)

3 tablespoons soy sauce

½ teaspoon sesame oil

½ teaspoon salt

¼ teaspoon ground black pepper

2 tablespoons sliced green onions, for garnishing

1. In a large wok or skillet, heat 1 tablespoon of the vegetable oil over medium heat. Once shimmering, add the eggs and cook, stirring continuously, for 2 to 3 minutes, until the eggs are cooked through. Transfer to a plate.

2. Wipe the skillet dry with paper towels. In the same wok or skillet, heat the remaining 1 tablespoon of oil over medium heat. Once shimmering, add the frozen vegetables. Cook, stirring often, for 3 to 5 minutes, until the vegetables are warmed through and most of the liquid in the pan has evaporated.

3. Add the cooked rice and stir until well combined. Add the soy sauce, sesame oil, salt, and pepper. Stir to combine, then add the egg mixture. Cook, stirring often, until the rice is warmed through and the coloring is consistent throughout, about 3 minutes.

4. Remove the wok from the heat and scoop the rice into a serving bowl. Sprinkle with the green onions and serve.

TIP

IF YOU HAVE DAY-OLD RICE, THIS IS THE TIME TO USE IT. **LEFTOVER RICE** IS ACTUALLY BETTER THAN FRESHLY COOKED RICE FOR THIS RECIPE, BECAUSE IT WILL HAVE LESS MOISTURE. THIS MEANS THE FINAL PRODUCT WILL BE LESS STICKY AND MORE **CRISPY.** IF YOU DON'T HAVE ANY DAY-OLD RICE, THEN SUB IN COOKED MICROWAVABLE RICE, FROZEN RICE, OR MAKE A NEW BATCH OF RICE.

LITTLE HELPING HANDS (3+)

Here is a special kitchen hack that anyone can do: Instead of cracking an egg on the corner of the pan or on the edge of the countertop, simply have your little helper hold the egg 6 inches (15 cm) above a plate and drop it! The drop makes a perfect break without shattering the membrane.

PORK AND SHRIMP WONTONS

MAKES 40 WONTONS

½ pound (227 g) ground pork

½ pound (227 g) raw jumbo (11 to 15 per pound) shrimp, peeled and deveined, finely chopped

2 green onions, sliced

2 tablespoons soy sauce

1 tablespoon granulated sugar

1 tablespoon sesame oil

1 tablespoon rice vinegar

2 teaspoons minced garlic

1 teaspoon salt

½ teaspoon ground black pepper

1 teaspoon minced, fresh ginger

1 package (12 ounces, or 340 g) wonton wrappers

Ponzu and/or sweet chili sauce, for serving (optional)

1. Fill a medium pot two-thirds of the way full with water and bring to a boil over medium heat. Reduce the heat to medium-low and maintain a low boil.

2. Meanwhile, in a large bowl, combine the pork, shrimp, green onions, soy sauce, sugar, sesame oil, rice vinegar, garlic, salt, pepper, and ginger. Stir until well combined.

3. Lay 1 wonton wrapper on a clean surface. Scoop 1 teaspoon of the filling onto the center of the wrapper. Run a wet finger along the entire perimeter of the wrapper. Bring the opposite sides of the wrapper up over the filling to meet one another and pinch together. Repeat with the remaining corners. Make sure the filling is entirely pinched within the wrapper. Repeat with the remaining wrappers and filling. You should have about 40 wontons.

4. Add 5 or 6 wontons at the same time to the boiling water and cook for 3 to 4 minutes, until they float to the top. Use a slotted spoon to transfer them to a plate.

5. Serve immediately with ponzu and/or sweet chili sauce (if using).

BIG KIDS IN THE KITCHEN (7+)

Allow your big kids to help wrap the wontons. Keep an eye out to make sure each one is tightly sealed.

CHOW MEIN

SERVES 6

1 package (16 ounces, or 454 g) spaghetti

3 tablespoons sesame oil

½ medium yellow onion, thinly sliced

½ medium head cabbage, thinly sliced

2 ribs celery, thinly sliced

2 tablespoons soy sauce

1 tablespoon oyster sauce

Sliced green onions, for garnishing

Sesame seeds, for garnishing

1. Bring a large pot of water to a boil over high heat. Add the spaghetti and cook according to package directions. Drain and set aside.

2. In a large wok or skillet, heat the sesame oil over medium heat. Once shimmering, add the onion, cabbage, and celery and cook, stirring often, for about 3 minutes, or until softened.

3. Add the spaghetti, soy sauce, and oyster sauce and toss. Cook for 1 to 2 minutes, until all the ingredients are incorporated and warmed.

4. Divide among 6 bowls, sprinkle with green onions and sesame seeds, and serve.

TWEENS ON THE SCENE (11+)

There are a lot of nifty kitchen tools, and one of them is a microwave pasta cooker. This plastic box can be used to quickly and easily cook pasta in one easy step, right in the microwave! Using one can be a little tricky because as you remove it from the microwave, the hot water can slosh around, but a tween with some hot pads should be able to manage!

AUSTRALIA WEEK

(AUSTRALIA DAY, JANUARY 26)

Australia Day, celebrated on January 26, is a summer holiday Down Under. January is the middle of summer, because Australia is in the Southern Hemisphere. Australia Day often involves beach barbecues, picnics, and delicious summer foods like grilled prawns. Here are some facts about Australia:

- If you live in the United States, Australia is one of the most distant places you can visit and has totally different wild animals too. For example, you might see a kangaroo in the wild in Australia, but you certainly wouldn't see one roaming around freely in the United States. A few other animals native to Australia are koalas, kookaburras, and Tasmanian devils. If you'd like to check these out in person (and can't visit Australia yourself), try your local zoo and enjoy Australian animals close to home.

- Before European settlers arrived, Australia was (and still is) home to Indigenous Aboriginal people with a rich history and culture. Visit your local library with your family to read more about Australian Aboriginals and share what you've learned with one another.

LAMINGTON

MAKES 12 LAMINGTONS

Cake

¾ cup (150 g) granulated sugar

½ cup (1 stick, or 115 g) salted butter, softened

1 teaspoon vanilla extract

2 large eggs

½ cup (120 ml) whole milk

4 teaspoons baking powder

2 cups (250 g) all-purpose flour

Chocolate Topping

3 tablespoons salted butter

½ cup (120 ml) whole milk

⅓ cup (30 g) unsweetened cocoa powder

2½ cups (313 g) confectioners' sugar

Strawberry Topping

3 tablespoons salted butter

½ cup (120 ml) whole milk

2½ cups (313 g) confectioners' sugar

¼ teaspoon strawberry extract

Pink food coloring

Coating

3 cups (260 g) shredded coconut

1. Preheat the oven to 350°F (180°C) and line a 9 by 9-inch (23 by 23 cm) baking dish with parchment paper.

2. **To make the cake:** In a large bowl, beat together the granulated sugar and butter with a hand or stand mixer on medium speed until light and fluffy, about 2 minutes. Add the vanilla, eggs, and milk and beat for 1 minute more. Add the baking powder and mix for 30 seconds. Keep the mixer set to medium and add the flour, a little at a time, until fully incorporated.

3. Pour the batter into the prepared pan and bake for 25 to 30 minutes, until a toothpick inserted in the center comes out clean. Let cool completely in the pan, about 1 hour. Gently remove the cake from the pan by pulling up on the parchment paper. Cut it into 12 pieces

4. **To make the chocolate and strawberry toppings:** For each topping, place the butter and milk in a heatproof bowl and microwave on high for 1 minute. Stir well to combine. For the chocolate topping, stir in the cocoa powder and confectioners' sugar until the mixture is smooth and uniform. For the strawberry topping, stir in the confectioners' sugar, strawberry extract, and food coloring until the mixture is smooth and uniform.

5. **To coat:** Add the shredded coconut to a shallow dish. Roll 6 cake pieces in the chocolate topping and the remaining 6 pieces in the strawberry topping, evenly coating all sides. Shake off any excess, then roll all pieces in the coconut, evenly coating all sides. Arrange on a parchment-lined baking sheet. Let rest for 30 minutes to set before serving.

TWEENS ON THE SCENE (11+)

If your tween loves making messes, get them involved in the decorating! Have them roll the cakes in the toppings and coconut.

LEMON, LIME, AND BITTERS (LLB)

SERVES 4

Ice

2 ounces (60 ml) fresh lemon juice

2 ounces (60 ml) fresh lime juice

16 dashes angostura bitters

16 ounces (480 ml) lemon-lime soda

4 lemon wheels, for garnishing

4 lime wheels, for garnishing

1. Fill a pitcher half-full with ice.

2. Add the lemon juice, lime juice, bitters, and lemon-lime soda. Gently stir to combine.

3. Top with the lemon and lime wheels and serve.

BIG KIDS IN THE KITCHEN (7+)

Squeezing lemons and limes isn't dangerous or tricky, but it does take some muscle! Bring in your big kids to get the juice out of that citrus!

BBQ SHRIMP

SERVES 4

1 cup (240 ml) olive oil

½ cup (120 ml) soy sauce

¼ cup (55 g) brown sugar

2 tablespoons fresh lemon juice

2 tablespoons minced garlic

1 tablespoon minced fresh ginger

1 teaspoon smoked paprika

¼ teaspoon ground black pepper

1 pound (454 g) raw jumbo (11 to 15 per pound) shrimp, peeled and deveined with tails on

Melted garlic butter, for serving (optional)

1. In a medium bowl, whisk together the olive oil, soy sauce, brown sugar, lemon juice, garlic, ginger, paprika, and pepper.

2. Add the shrimp and toss to coat. Cover and refrigerate the shrimp for 1 hour to marinate.

3. Preheat a grill to medium-high or a grill pan over medium-high heat. Place the shrimp directly on the grill grates or add to the grill pan and cook for 2 to 4 minutes per side, until the shrimp are opaque and reach an internal temperature of 145°F (60°C). Remove from the heat and serve immediately with garlic butter (if using) for dipping.

NOTE

IN THE UNITED STATES, WE MOSTLY HAVE SHRIMP AVAILABLE IN THE GROCERY STORE, BUT IN AUSTRALIA, PRAWNS ARE MORE COMMON. SHRIMP AND PRAWNS ARE RELATIVES, BUT DIFFER IN BODY COMPOSITION AND FLAVOR, WITH SHRIMP BEING SALTIER AND PRAWNS SWEETER.

BUDDING SOUS-CHEFS (17+)

Grilling is a culinary quest best suited for those 17+. Head outside and demonstrate how to fire up the grill. Then, cut the heat and supervise as your budding sous-chef gives it a whirl. Assign all grilling activities to your new fire tender, but secretly observe from a few feet away so that if anything goes wrong, they can ask you for help.

AMERICAN SOUL FOOD WEEK

(BLACK HISTORY MONTH, FEBRUARY)

RECIPES

SWEET TEA 33

SLOW COOKER MAC AND CHEESE 34

BANANA PUDDING 36

February is Black History Month, a perfect time to learn about and celebrate Black culture and history.

This week, visit your local library to discover their Black History Month section. Find books that match your reading level to learn more about Black history. Here are some suggestions:

- **THE STORY OF RUBY BRIDGES BY ROBERT COLES.** This book tells the story of Ruby Bridges, the first Black child to desegregate a white elementary school in Louisiana.

- **HIDDEN FIGURES: TRUE STORIES OF AFRICAN AMERICAN WOMEN WHO HELPED LAUNCH SPACE MISSIONS BY MARGOT LEE SHETTERLY.** This book is now a popular movie. Consider reading the book or watching the film with your family!

SWEET TEA

SERVES 6

1 cup (200 g) granulated sugar
⅛ teaspoon baking soda
6 black tea bags
4 cups (960 ml) cold water
Lemon wedges, for serving

1. In a small pot or tea kettle, bring 4 cups (960 ml) of water to a boil. Meanwhile, add the sugar and baking soda to a large pitcher. Pour the boiling water over the sugar mixture. Stir well to combine. Add the tea bags and steep for 10 minutes. Remove the tea bags from the water and discard.

2. Pour in the cold water, stir, and let the mixture chill in the refrigerator for at least 1 hour.

3. Fill a glass with ice and pour the tea over the ice. Serve with lemon wedges and enjoy.

4. Leftover sweet tea can be kept in the refrigerator up to 3 days.

LITTLE HELPING HANDS (3+)

Stirring the sweet tea is a job anyone can do! Grab your littlest helper and a big wooden spoon and let them mix everything together.

SLOW COOKER MAC AND CHEESE

SERVES 6

1 box (16 ounces, or 454 g) elbow pasta

½ cup (1 stick, or 115 g) salted butter, cubed

1 teaspoon salt

½ teaspoon ground black pepper

1 package (16 ounces, or 454 g) shredded sharp cheddar cheese

1 can (5 ounces, or 148 ml) evaporated milk

2 large eggs

2 cups (480 ml) whole milk

1 can (10.5 ounces, or 300 g) condensed cheddar cheese soup

Cooked, crumbled bacon, for serving (optional)

1. Cook the elbow pasta to al dente according to package directions. Drain and transfer to a 6-quart slow cooker. Set to low and stir in the butter. Once melted, add the salt, pepper, cheddar, and evaporated milk.

2. In a medium bowl, whisk together the eggs, milk, and soup until combined. Pour the mixture into the slow cooker and stir until incorporated.

3. Cover and cook on low, stirring occasionally, for 2 hours and 30 minutes to 3 hours, until the cheese is melted and everything is hot. Sprinkle with bacon (if using) and serve. Leftovers can be stored in an airtight container in the refrigerator for up to 4 days.

LITTLE HELPING HANDS (3+)

Little helpers can assist by dumping the egg mixture into the slow cooker when it's time. After your little has done their part, you can give the mixture a good stir, put the lid on, and then while the dish is cooking, grab one of the books listed in this chapter and read it together as a family.

BANANA PUDDING

SERVES 12

2 packages (3.4 ounces, or 96 g, each) vanilla instant pudding mix

4 cups (960 ml) whole milk

4 ripe bananas, peeled and sliced

1 box (11 ounces, or 310 g) vanilla wafers

1 container (8 ounces, or 227 g) frozen whipped topping, thawed

1. In a large bowl, whisk together the pudding mix and milk. Place in the refrigerator to chill for 15 minutes.

2. Scoop one-third of the pudding mixture into a 9 by 13-inch (23 by 23 cm) baking dish. Spread into an even layer, taking care to make sure the bottom of the dish is completely covered with pudding.

3. Arrange one-third of the banana slices in a single layer across the top of the pudding. Next, arrange one-third of the vanilla wafers in a single layer on top of the banana slices. Repeat two more times with the remaining pudding, banana slices, and vanilla wafers.

4. Scoop the whipped topping onto the top of the last layer and smooth across the entire surface to cover the wafers completely. Place in the refrigerator to chill and set for 1 hour.

5. To serve, cut into squares or simply scoop out with a big serving spoon.

BIG KIDS IN THE KITCHEN (7+)

Your big kids can make this entire recipe! The banana can be cut using a safety knife so little fingers can be protected. Other than that, it's just about mixing and assembling, so sit back and watch them create a masterpiece.

MOROCCO WEEK

(ALMOND BLOSSOM FESTIVAL)

Nestled in North Africa, Morocco is renowned for its vibrant mosaics and colorful textiles. The country also boasts a unique cooking vessel called a tagine. Shaped like a cone resting on a shallow dish, the tagine traps steam and juices, ensuring moist and flavorful dishes.

Early February in Morocco brings the enchanting Almond Blossom Festival, where almond trees burst into bloom, painting the landscape in shades of white and pink. Almonds are a cherished part of Moroccan culture and cuisine, which you'll discover in the following recipes:

- **CHICKEN TAGINE** is a slow-simmered stew. For this recipe, you can use a tagine or a Dutch oven. If you have a tagine, talk to your kids about how this cooking method dates all the way back to the ninth century.

- **MSEMEN** (pronounced like "messy men") is a traditionally savory flatbread, but try dusting it in cinnamon sugar instead of semolina flour for a sweet version.

- **AMLOU** is a delicious dip that is much like almond butter. This snack would go great in a small, plastic container in a lunch box.

CHICKEN TAGINE

SERVES 6

1 tablespoon olive oil

4 bone-in, skin-on chicken thighs (4 to 5 ounces, or 115 to 145 g, each)

2 teaspoons salt

1 teaspoon ground black pepper

1 large yellow onion, chopped

1 teaspoon minced garlic

1 teaspoon ground ginger

1 teaspoon ground cinnamon

1 teaspoon ground turmeric

4 cups (960 ml) chicken broth

½ cup (65 g) chopped dried apricots

¼ cup (35 g) golden raisins

1 whole lemon, peeled, seeded, and diced

Rice or Msemen (see page 40), for serving

Fresh parsley leaves, for serving (optional)

1. In a large Dutch oven or tagine, heat the olive oil over medium heat. Sprinkle both sides of the chicken thighs with the salt and pepper and place, skin sides down, in the hot oil. Allow to cook for about 2 minutes, then flip and cook for 2 minutes more, or until both sides are nicely browned. Transfer to a plate.

2. Add the onion and garlic to the same pot the chicken was cooked in and cook for about 5 minutes, or until softened. Stir in the ginger, cinnamon, and turmeric and cook for 1 minute more. Pour in the chicken broth, and sprinkle in the apricots, raisins, and lemon pieces. Bring to a boil over medium heat.

3. Return the chicken to the pot, gently nestling it into the sauce until it is halfway submerged. Reduce the heat to medium-low, cover, and let simmer for 40 to 45 minutes, until the chicken is cooked through and reads 165°F (75°C) on an instant-read thermometer.

4. Serve over rice or with msemen and garnish with parsley (if using).

BUDDING SOUS-CHEFS (17+)

Cooking chicken is serious business since raw chicken can carry harmful bacteria, and no one wants that! Let your budding sous-chef use a meat thermometer to check the temperature of the chicken to ensure it is thoroughly cooked and safe to consume.

MSEMEN

MAKES 8 MSEMEN

3 cups (375 g) all-purpose flour, plus more for dusting

1 cup (180 g) semolina flour, divided

1½ teaspoons active dry yeast

1 teaspoon granulated sugar

1½ teaspoons salt

1½ cups (360 ml) warm water (120°F, or 50°C)

Nonstick cooking spray

¾ cup (1½ sticks, or 170 g) butter, melted, divided

½ cup (120 ml) vegetable oil

Chicken Tagine (page 38), for serving (optional)

TWEENS ON THE SCENE (11+)

Show your tween how to fold each of the msemen dough slices and then watch proudly while they do the rest of the folding.

1. In a large bowl, stir together the all-purpose flour, ½ cup (90 g) of the semolina flour, yeast, sugar, and salt. Stir in the warm water and mix just until the dough comes together, then use your hands or a stand mixer fitted with a dough hook to knead until the dough is smooth and elastic, 5 to 10 minutes.

2. Grease a large bowl with nonstick cooking spray. Form the dough into a ball, place it in the prepared bowl, and cover with plastic wrap greased with cooking spray. Allow to rest in a warm area until doubled in size, about 1 hour.

3. Dust a large work surface with all-purpose flour and turn the dough out onto the flour. Cut the dough into 8 equal wedges (like pizza slices). Working with one slice at a time, use your hands to roll each into a ball. Use a rolling pin to roll out a ⅛-inch-thick (3 mm) square from each of the dough balls. The squares should be about 14 inches (36 cm) wide and long. Brush the entire surfaces of the squares with ½ cup (1 stick, or 115 g) of the melted butter and sprinkle with ¼ cup (45 g) of the semolina flour.

4. Fold a dough square into thirds, bringing the top third down and the bottom third up. Then, fold the remaining strip into thirds, bringing the left third over, then the right third inward. You should finish with a small square packet. Brush the top with more melted butter and sprinkle with a little more semolina flour. Fold the remaining dough squares, then brush them with the remaining ¼ cup (½ stick, or 55 g) melted butter and sprinkle with the remaining ¼ cup (45 g) semolina flour, placing the packets onto a baking sheet in a single layer.

5. In a large skillet, heat the vegetable oil over medium heat. Once shimmering, cook 1 or 2 packets at a time, undisturbed, for 2 to 3 minutes, until golden. Flip and cook 2 to 3 minutes more, until equally golden and cooked through. Transfer to a paper towel–lined plate.

6. Serve with chicken tagine (if using).

AMLOU

SERVES 6

3½ cups (490 g) whole raw almonds

3 tablespoons almond oil

¼ cup (60 ml) honey

¼ teaspoon salt

Apple slices or crackers, for serving

1. Preheat the oven to 375°F (190°C). Arrange the almonds in a single layer on a baking sheet and bake for 15 to 30 minutes, until toasted and fragrant, stirring halfway through. Transfer the almonds to a heatproof bowl and let cool for 30 minutes, or until completely cool.

2. In a blender or food processor, process the almonds 5 to 10 minutes, until a smooth paste forms. Add the almond oil, honey, and salt and blend for 1 minute more.

3. Scoop the butter into a serving bowl and serve with apple slices or crackers. Leftovers can be stored in an airtight jar in a cool dry place up to 2 weeks.

LITTLE HELPING HANDS (3+)

Since we are letting the almonds cool completely before adding them to the food processor, your littlest helpers can move the almonds to the food processor and (once an adult has secured the lid and turned on the processor) monitor the progress of blending them. It is like magic watching the nuts transform into bits, then a goopy paste, and finally a smooth paste!

VALENTINE WEEK

(FEBRUARY 14)

Valentine's Day, once a religious observance, has evolved into simply a celebration of love. It's a day to express affection for those we cherish, often accompanied by sweet treats like chocolate.

In American schools, a common Valentine's Day tradition involves exchanging cards or notes with classmates, sometimes including small gifts or treats. Consider incorporating a similar activity within your own family. Instead of store-bought cards, create personalized valentines for one another. In the days leading up to Valentine's Day, encourage family members to gather information about each other's preferences and interests to tailor their cards accordingly. For example, I love doughnuts. One year my daughter made me a card with a big pink doughnut on the front that said "Mommy (hearts) Doughnuts," and it was perfect!

Regardless of how you choose to celebrate, the red-themed treats and snacks in the pages that follow are sure to add a special touch to your day.

HEART-SHAPED BRUSCHETTA

MAKES 4 BRUSCHETTA

4 thick slices sourdough bread

2 tablespoons olive oil

1 teaspoon garlic powder

2 ripe Roma tomatoes, finely diced

2 tablespoons finely chopped fresh basil, plus more for garnishing

1 tablespoon balsamic glaze

½ teaspoon salt

¼ teaspoon ground black pepper

1. Preheat the oven to 400°F (200°C). Line a baking sheet with parchment paper.

2. Use a large heart-shaped cookie cutter to cut a heart out of each slice of bread.

3. Brush each heart with olive oil and sprinkle with garlic powder. Arrange the hearts on the prepared baking sheet in a single layer and bake for 3 to 5 minutes, until golden brown. Remove from the oven.

4. In a medium bowl, stir together the Roma tomatoes, basil, balsamic glaze, salt, and pepper.

5. Spread each piece of toast with a heaping spoonful of the tomato mixture. Use the back of the spoon to smooth out the tomato mixture into a uniform layer.

6. Set the finished pieces on a serving platter and garnish with more basil.

LITTLE HELPING HANDS (3+)

While cutting ingredients is reserved for bigger kids and adults, little helpers can add all the pre-cut ingredients to the mixing bowl, give it a stir, and then assemble all the toasts themselves!

STRAWBERRY RED VELVET WHOOPIE PIES

MAKES 12 WHOOPIE PIES

Red Velvet Cake

Nonstick cooking spray

1 box (15.25 ounces, or 432 g) red velvet cake mix

½ cup (120 ml) vegetable oil

3 large eggs

Cream Cheese Buttercream

1 package (8 ounces, or 227 g) cream cheese, softened

½ cup (1 stick, or 115 g) salted butter, softened

4 cups (500 g) confectioners' sugar

2 teaspoons vanilla extract

Strawberry Buttercream

1 cup (2 sticks, or 230 g) salted butter, softened

4 cups (500 g) confectioners' sugar

¼ cup (60 ml) strawberry syrup puree

Assembly

1 cup (190 g) assorted red, white, and pink sprinkles

6 strawberries, hulled and cut in half

1. To make the red velvet cake: Preheat the oven to 350°F (180°C). Spray two 12-divot whoopie pie pans (or a jumbo muffin tin) with nonstick cooking spray.

2. In a large bowl, stir together the cake mix, oil, eggs, and 1½ cups (360 ml) of water. Divide the batter between the whoopie pie divots (if using a jumbo muffin tin, only fill the cups with ½ inch, or 12 mm, of batter) and bake for 10 to 15 minutes, until a toothpick inserted into the center comes out clean. Let cool in the pan for 10 minutes. Transfer the cakes to a wire cooling rack and let cool completely, about 1 hour.

3. To make the cream cheese and strawberry buttercreams: For the cream cheese buttercream, in the bowl of a stand mixer fitted with the whisk attachment, beat the cream cheese and ½ cup (115 g) butter on low for 2 minutes, or until smooth. Add the sugar and vanilla and beat for 2 minutes more. For the strawberry buttercream, in the bowl of a stand mixer fitted with a whisk attachment, beat the 1 cup (230 g) butter on medium for 2 minutes, or until smooth. Add the sugar and strawberry puree and beat for 2 minutes more. Scoop each buttercream into separate piping bags fitted with large star tips.

4. To assemble: Place one cake round, face down, on a plate or cutting board. Swirl the cream cheese buttercream across the entire surface of the cake and top with a second piece of cake. Press 1 tablespoon of sprinkles into the sides of the frosting. Finish with a swirl of strawberry buttercream and add a strawberry half on top. Repeat with the remaining cakes and buttercreams. Serve immediately or refrigerate in an airtight container for up to 3 days.

BIG KIDS IN THE KITCHEN (7+)

Big kids can don some disposable kitchen gloves and press the sprinkles into the buttercream on each of the cakes. Gloves can be especially helpful for kids with sensory needs.

LOVE POTION FLOATS

MAKES 4 FLOATS

8 scoops vanilla ice cream

24 ounces (680 ml) strawberry-flavored soda

Canned whipped cream

4 teaspoons red-colored sugar sprinkles

1. Add 2 scoops of vanilla ice cream to a plastic cup or glass.

2. Slowly pour in 6 ounces (170 ml) of strawberry soda, then top with whipped cream and 1 teaspoon of sprinkles.

3. Repeat with the remaining ingredients until you have 4 floats. Serve immediately.

TWEENS ON THE SCENE (11+)

The soda needs to be added slowly and carefully so it won't fizz over. Ask your tween to add the soda to the cups gradually and gently.

FISH WEEK

(LENT)

Lent, a period of reflection and repentance observed by many Christians, begins on Ash Wednesday and concludes on Easter. During this period (40 weekdays), believers often focus more intently on their faith and may choose to abstain from certain indulgences. A common practice is giving up red meat, leading to an increased consumption of fish dishes.

While Lent is a religious observance, anyone can enjoy these delicious seafood options year-round. Here are some fishy facts:

- Did you know that a single tuna can weigh up to 2,000 pounds (907 kg)? It's a little crazy when you think that it often comes in a 5-ounce (140 g) can. This fish can also swim at speeds of more than 50 miles per hour (80 km/h) and migrate thousands of miles.

- To ensure the long-term sustainability of fish populations, it's crucial to support responsible fishing practices. Fishers can use modern technology to avoid accidental catches of endangered species and protect critical habitats. By choosing sustainably sourced seafood, you can contribute to the preservation of marine ecosystems for future generations. Not sure where to start? The Monterey Bay Aquarium has put together guides to help.

AIR FRYER SALMON

SERVES 6

1 skin-on salmon fillet
  (2½ pounds, or 1.2 kg)
½ cup (120 ml) mayonnaise
1 tablespoon salt
1 tablespoon garlic powder
2 teaspoons Italian seasoning
Lemon wedges, for serving

1. Preheat an air fryer to 400°F (200°C).

2. Meanwhile, cut the salmon into 6 equal pieces. Brush each piece on the top and sides with the mayonnaise and sprinkle with the salt, garlic powder, and Italian seasoning.

3. Cook undisturbed for 10 to 15 minutes, until the internal temperature at the thickest part of the fish reaches 145°F (60°C). Serve with lemon wedges for squeezing.

BIG KIDS IN THE KITCHEN (7+)

Brushing mayonnaise on fish is easy, satisfying, and fun! Enlist your big kids to help and ask them to sprinkle on the seasonings as well. In fact, this recipe can be made with just about any seasoning blend in place of the Italian seasoning. My kids love garlic and herb, dill pickle, or herbes de Provence the best. Let your big kid choose, if they'd like!

TUNA ROLLS

SERVES 6

1 can (5 ounces, or 140 g) tuna in water, drained

2 tablespoons mayonnaise

2 tablespoons pickle relish

½ teaspoon salt

½ teaspoon ground black pepper

½ teaspoon lemon pepper seasoning

6 slices white bread, crusts removed

1. In a small bowl, stir together the tuna, mayonnaise, relish, salt, black, pepper, and lemon pepper until combined.

2. Arrange the bread in a single layer on a large cutting board. Depending on the size of the board, you may need to work in batches. Use a rolling pin to flatten the bread until it is ⅛-inch (3 mm) thick.

3. Spread the tuna filling among the 6 slices of bread. Working with one slice at a time, start at the shorter end of the bread and roll the bread onto itself into a tight jelly roll. Roll each tightly in plastic wrap and refrigerate for 20 minutes.

4. To serve, remove the plastic wrap and either eat as is (in "burrito" form) or cut into 1-inch-wide (2.5 cm) pinwheels and serve.

BIG KIDS IN THE KITCHEN (7+)

This entire recipe can be prepared by a big kid, aside from draining the tuna (can lids can be very sharp!) and cutting the crust off the bread. Simply do these steps for them and allow them to take over the rest!

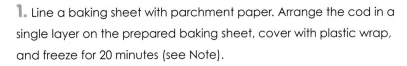

FISH STICKS

SERVES 4

1 pound (454 g) fresh cod

6 cups (1.4 L) vegetable oil, for frying

2 teaspoons salt

1 teaspoon ground black pepper

2 large eggs

½ cup (120 ml) buttermilk

1 cup (80 g) panko bread crumbs

1 cup (125 g) all-purpose flour

1 tablespoon garlic powder

1 teaspoon paprika

Favorite dipping sauce, for serving

NOTE
FREEZING THE FISH A LITTLE BIT WILL MAKE IT EASIER TO WORK WITH

1. Line a baking sheet with parchment paper. Arrange the cod in a single layer on the prepared baking sheet, cover with plastic wrap, and freeze for 20 minutes (see Note).

2. Attach a deep-fry thermometer to the side of a large, deep, heavy pot. Add the oil and heat to 350°F (180°C) over medium heat.

3. Cut the fish into pieces about 2 inches (5 cm) long and ½ inch (12 mm) wide. Sprinkle all over with salt and pepper.

4. In a shallow dish or bowl, whisk together the eggs and buttermilk. In a second shallow dish or bowl, stir together the bread crumbs, flour, garlic powder, and paprika.

5. Working one at a time, dip each fish piece in the egg batter, turn to coat, and allow the excess to drip off. Then, roll in the flour mixture and gently press to adhere.

6. Carefully add the fish to the hot oil, working in batches of 3 to 5 sticks at a time. Cook, undisturbed, for 1 to 3 minutes, until the exterior is golden brown and the internal temperature of the fish reaches 145°F (60°C). Transfer to a paper towel–lined plate. Repeat with the remaining fish sticks.

7. Let the sticks cool for 10 minutes before serving with your favorite dipping sauce.

BIG KIDS IN THE KITCHEN (7+)

Have your big kid don some disposable gloves and take charge of the dredging stations. It is like playing in a sandbox in the kitchen!

CHEESE WEEK

Cheese is enjoyed worldwide. It's typically made by curdling milk and then separating the curds from the whey. The type of milk, additional ingredients, aging process, and other factors influence the final cheese's flavor, texture, and appearance.

This week, explore the gourmet cheese section of your local grocery store. You'll be amazed by the variety of cheeses available from around the world, from classic cheddar to exotic blue cheeses. Pay attention to the names, colors, shapes, and sizes of different cheeses.

Grab a few varieties to eat with crackers or to slip into the middle of a grilled cheese sandwich. While a simple combination of cheddar and mozzarella is delicious in a grilled cheese, don't be afraid to experiment with different varieties. Imagine the flavor possibilities with Gouda, Swiss, or even adding grilled onions. The world of grilled cheese is your oyster!

TABLE-SIZE NACHOS

SERVES 6

1 bag (13 ounces, or 369 g) tortilla chips

1 can (10.5 ounces, or 298 g) nacho cheese sauce, warmed

1 can (15 ounces, or 425 g) black beans, rinsed and drained

1 large tomato, diced

2 cups (390 g) precooked shredded chicken, warmed

1 package (8 ounces, or 227 g) shredded Mexican-style cheese

1 avocado, peeled, pitted, and chopped

Salsa

Sour cream

Fresh cilantro leaves

1. Spread aluminum foil in a large swath on the middle of your kitchen or dining room table.

2. Dump the entire bag of chips onto the foil and spread the chips out a bit. Drizzle with the nacho cheese sauce (yes, directly on the foil on your table; this will be fun, I swear!), then top with the black beans, tomatoes, chicken, cheese, and avocado.

3. Add as much salsa, sour cream, and cilantro as your family likes.

4. Everyone dig in! Eat directly off the table. When you're done, simply roll up the aluminum foil and throw away all the mess.

LITTLE HELPING HANDS (3+)

Kids **LOVE** to make a mess, but they love to make one even more when they are **ASKED** and **ALLOWED** to make that mess! Let them sprinkle the beans, tomatoes, chicken, and cheese all over the nacho-ed chips, and they can even leave off some ingredients from certain sections to customize the nachos for everyone! Your little helping hands will be shocked to see dinner spread out over the whole table!

FONDUE

SERVES 6

2 cups (220 g) shredded Gruyère cheese

2 cups (230 g) shredded Swiss cheese

2 tablespoons cornstarch

1 cup (240 ml) chicken broth

¼ teaspoon fresh lemon juice

1 teaspoon garlic powder

½ teaspoon ground black pepper

¼ teaspoon paprika

Optional Dippers

1 small loaf sourdough bread, cut into cubes

2 cups new potatoes, cooked

Baby carrots

Apples, cut into cubes

1. To a zip-top plastic bag, add the Gruyère cheese, Swiss cheese, and cornstarch and shake until the cheese is well coated with the cornstarch.

2. In a medium pot, heat the chicken broth and lemon juice over medium heat for 3 to 5 minutes, until simmering. Slowly add the cheese, one handful at a time, stirring to incorporate each handful. Cook, stirring continuously, until the cheese is melted.

3. Remove the pot from the heat and stir in the garlic powder, pepper, and paprika. Transfer the melted cheese to a fondue pot and light the heat source (see Tip).

4. Skewer a dipper with a fondue poker, fork, or wooden skewer and dip it into the cheese. Blow on the cheese to cool it slightly before eating it.

LITTLE HELPING HANDS (3+)

Grab a little helper and get them to shake up the cheese and cornstarch in the zip-top plastic bag. It is helpful and lots of fun!

TIP

THERE ARE SEVERAL TYPES OF FONDUE POTS, BUT THE MOST COMMON ARE ELECTRIC (THAT YOU CAN PLUG IN TO HEAT) OR FLAME (A POT HEATED BY A CHAFING FUEL CANISTER). EITHER ARE EASY TO USE, WORK GREAT FOR FONDUE, AND CAN BE FOUND ONLINE.

GRILLED CHEESE

MAKES 4 SANDWICHES

2 slices brioche bread

2 tablespoons mayonnaise

2 tablespoons salted butter

¼ cup (30 g) shredded cheddar cheese

¼ cup (30 g) shredded mozzarella cheese

1. Lay the slices of bread on a work surface and spread the mayonnaise on one side of each slice.

2. In a medium skillet with a lid, melt the butter over medium heat. Place one slice of bread in the pan, mayonnaise side down. Evenly sprinkle the cheddar cheese, then the mozzarella cheese across the bread. Add the second slice of bread, mayonnaise side up, onto the cheese.

3. Cover with the lid and cook for about 3 minutes, or until the bottom of the sandwich is golden brown. Flip, cover, and cook 1 to 3 minutes more, until the cheese is melted and the bottom is golden brown.

4. Transfer to a plate, cut in half, and serve.

TWEENS ON THE SCENE (11+)

If you have a grilled-cheese maker, your tween can easily make grilled cheese sandwiches all by themself. These makers are typically inexpensive from online stores and remove the need to flip the sandwich in a pan. This makes it easy, twice as fast, and safer!

INDIA WEEK

(HOLI FESTIVAL)

Holi Festival, also known as the "Festival of Colors," celebrates the arrival of spring. One of the most exciting parts of the holiday is when everyone throws colored powders at each other! If you want to try this at home, be sure to do it outside and in clothes that can get messy. This week, if you have the time, try to serve all your recipes together.

First, make some NAAN, which is a bread that is great for scooping up curries (the naan can be made one to two days in advance if you can't do all the cooking in one day).

Then, make an Indian-inspired COCONUT CHICKEN CURRY packed with fresh vegetables and exotic flavors like garam masala. Garam masala is a spice blend that typically includes cardamom, cinnamon, cloves, coriander, and cumin. Most grocery stores carry it, or it can be ordered online.

Lastly, make a MANGO LASSI, a refreshing drink that really beats the heat on hot summer days.

MANGO LASSI

MAKES 4 LASSI

4 cups (700 g) frozen mango chunks

4 cups (960 ml) plain yogurt

2 cups (480 ml) whole milk

½ cup (120 ml) honey

Dash of cardamom

1. In a blender, process the mango, yogurt, milk, honey, and cardamom on medium speed for about 2 minutes, or until smooth.

2. Pour into 4 glasses and serve.

LITTLE HELPING HANDS (3+)

Let your little hands add the ingredients to the blender and help them put the lid on and press the buttons. If you have any twisty straws, let your little helper pick one for everyone in the family!

NAAN

MAKES 6 NAAN

¾ cup (180 ml) warm water (120°F, or 50°C)

2 teaspoons granulated sugar

1 teaspoon quick-rise yeast

3 tablespoons plain yogurt

2 tablespoons olive oil, plus more for greasing and cooking

2 cups (250 g) all-purpose flour, plus more for dusting

1 teaspoon salt

½ teaspoon baking powder

6 teaspoons vegetable oil, plus more for greasing

6 teaspoons salted butter, softened

1 tablespoon flaky salt

Slow Cooker Coconut Curry Chicken (opposite), for serving (optional)

BIG KIDS IN THE KITCHEN (7+)

Have your big kid roll out the dough slices into teardrop shapes.

1. In a small bowl, stir together the water and sugar. Sprinkle in the yeast and stir again. Set aside for 10 minutes for the yeast to bloom.

2. Add the yogurt and olive oil to the yeast mixture and stir gently to combine.

3. In a large bowl, use an electric or stand mixer set to low speed and mix the flour, salt, and baking powder. With the mixer on, slowly pour in the yeast mixture and mix until combined.

4. Knead until the dough comes together, about 3 minutes. (The dough can be kneaded by hand or with a stand mixer fitted with a dough hook. If using a stand mixer, set the speed to low.)

5. Transfer the dough to a bowl greased with vegetable oil. Also grease one side of a piece of plastic wrap, then cover the bowl with the prepared wrap, greased side down. Allow to rise in a warm place for about 45 minutes, or until the dough has doubled in size.

6. Turn the dough out onto a lightly floured surface. Use your hands to slightly flatten the ball into a disk. Use a sharp knife to cut the dough, like a pizza, into 6 equal slices. Working with one piece at a time, use a floured rolling pin to flatten it into a teardrop shape about ⅛ inch (3 mm) thick.

7. Heat a large skillet over medium-high heat and drizzle with 1 teaspoon of vegetable oil. Once the oil shimmers, add a piece of dough and cook for 1 to 2 minutes, until slightly charred. Flip and cook 1 to 2 minutes more, until evenly charred and cooked through. Transfer to a plate. Repeat with the remaining dough and vegetable oil.

8. Spread 1 teaspoon of the butter across each piece of bread and sprinkle with flaky salt. Serve with coconut curry chicken (if using).

SLOW COOKER COCONUT CHICKEN CURRY

SERVES 6

3 boneless, skinless chicken breasts (1½ pounds, or 680 g, total), cubed

1 large yellow onion, halved

1 large green bell pepper, cored, seeded, and halved

1 can (13.5 ounces, or 400 ml) unsweetened coconut milk

1 can (6 ounces, or 170 g) tomato paste

1 tablespoon curry powder

1 tablespoon garam masala

2 teaspoons minced garlic

2 teaspoons salt

2 tablespoons cold water

1½ tablespoons cornstarch

Rice, for serving

Naan (opposite), for serving (optional)

1. Place the chicken in a slow cooker set to low.

2. Meanwhile, in a food processor or blender set to low speed, process the onion, bell pepper, coconut milk, tomato paste, curry powder, garam masala, garlic, and salt for about 2 minutes, or until smooth.

3. Pour the coconut-milk mixture over the chicken and stir to combine. Cover and cook on low for 5 hours.

4. In a small bowl, whisk together the cold water and cornstarch. Drizzle into the slow cooker while continuously stirring. Let cook for 1 hour more, then serve over rice with naan (if using).

TWEENS ON THE SCENE (11+)

Slow cookers are great kitchen tools because they are safer than a skillet that can splatter or an oven that can burn. Direct your tween to keep their paws off the outside of the slow cooker, as it can get warm. Then, ask them to add all the ingredients to the slow cooker and stir. They may also like assembling the finished product to serve to the whole family.

PIE WEEK

(PI DAY, MARCH 14)

RECIPES

APPLE PIE 63
CHICKEN POT PIE 64
PIE SHAKES 66

Pies can be basically any filling encased in a crust, and while it may be easy to think *Pie! Apple Pie! American!*, pie actually has roots in the Middle Ages, dating back to the thirteenth and fourteenth centuries. During this time, many foods were encased in a crust to extend their shelf life. Interestingly, the outer crust was often used only for preservation and not eaten.

Seemingly growing in popularity every year, March 14 is an unofficial "Pi Day" celebrating the number Pi (~3.14) on March 14 (3/14). Baking nerds and math nerds combine forces on the perfect day! It is also excellent because pi is the mathematical constant representing the ratio of a circle's circumference to its diameter, and pies are often circles!

But pies come in all shapes and sizes, and this chapter has one round, one rectangular, and one in a glass cup! So enjoy your Pi Day and your Pie Week loving all kinds of shapes!

APPLE PIE

SERVES 8

Nonstick cooking spray

2 refrigerated piecrusts
(9 inches, or 23 cm, each),
at room temperature

6 large Granny Smith apples,
peeled, cored, and thinly
sliced

3 tablespoons all-purpose flour,
plus more for dusting

½ cup (1 stick, or 115 g) salted
butter

½ cup (100 g) granulated sugar

½ cup (110 g) brown sugar

Whipped cream or ice cream,
for serving

BIG KIDS IN THE KITCHEN (7+)

With a pizza cutter, your big kid can easily cut the dough into strips.

1. Preheat the oven to 425°F (220°C). Grease a 9-inch (23 cm) pie plate with nonstick cooking spray.

2. Press one of the piecrusts into the bottom and all the way up the sides of the prepared dish. Spread the apple slices on the crust.

3. Lightly dust a work surface with flour, then unroll the second piecrust and cut it into 9 strips (about 1 inch, or 2.5 cm, wide each). Now create a lattice for the top of the pie: Place 4 of the strips onto the apples, evenly spaced. Fold back the first and third strips (so they are folded in half), then place one of the remaining strips perpendicular to the first strips. Lay the first and third strips back down, then fold back the second and fourth strips back to add the next perpendicular strip. Then again with the first and third. Spin the pie around and repeat with the opposite side and the remaining 2 strips. Crimp the edges of the crust with a fork to keep everything together.

4. In a small saucepan over medium heat, melt the butter. Stir in the 3 tablespoons flour and cook for 1 to 2 minutes more, stirring constantly. Stir in the granulated sugar, brown sugar, and ¼ cup (60 ml) of water and bring to a boil over medium heat. Reduce the heat to low and let simmer for 5 minutes. The liquid should be slightly thickened but not thick enough to coat the back of a spoon.

5. Pour the hot sugar mixture over the lattice crust, working in a circular motion from the inside out to equally coat the whole piecrust. The mixture will seep into the holes and fill the pie.

6. Bake for 15 minutes. Reduce the oven temperature to 350°F (180°C) and bake for an additional 35 to 45 minutes, until the top is golden brown and the filling is bubbly.

7. Serve either warm or cold with whipped cream or ice cream.

CHICKEN POT PIE

SERVES 8

Nonstick cooking spray

¼ cup (½ stick, or 55 g) salted butter

1 medium yellow onion, diced

½ cup (70 g) diced carrots

½ cup (50 g) diced celery

⅔ cup (90 g) frozen peas

½ cup (65 g) all-purpose flour

1 tablespoon dried parsley

½ teaspoon dried thyme

2 cups (480 ml) chicken broth

⅔ cup (165 ml) half-and-half

3 cups (585 g) cubed cooked chicken

1 teaspoon salt

½ teaspoon ground black pepper

1 can (16.3 ounces, or 462 g) flaky refrigerated biscuits

1 large egg yolk

1. Preheat the oven to 350°F (180°C). Grease a 7 by 11-inch (17 by 28 cm) baking dish with nonstick cooking spray.

2. In a large skillet over medium heat, melt the butter. Once bubbling, add the onion, carrots, and celery and cook for about 15 minutes, stirring often, until soft.

3. Add the peas, flour, parsley, and thyme and cook for another 5 minutes. Whisk in the chicken broth and half-and-half and cook for 2 minutes more. Gently stir in the chicken, salt, and pepper until combined.

4. Spoon the chicken mixture into the prepared dish and place the biscuits evenly across the top. In a small bowl, beat the egg yolk with 1 tablespoon of water and brush the egg wash over the top of the biscuits.

5. Bake for 20 to 25 minutes, until the filling is bubbly and biscuits are cooked through and golden brown. Serve immediately.

BIG KIDS IN THE KITCHEN (7+)

You know what one of the scariest jobs in the kitchen is? Opening the can of biscuits!!! It takes real guts and fearlessness. Have your big kid tackle the challenge. Here is a tip: once they've ripped the opener tab almost all the way, have them tap the can lightly on the edge of a countertop until the can pops!

PIE SHAKES

MAKES 4 SHAKES

1 cup (240 ml) whole milk

1 cup (240 ml) apple juice

4 scoops vanilla ice cream

1 teaspoon ground cinnamon

½ teaspoon ground nutmeg

¼ teaspoon ground allspice

1. In a blender, blend the milk, apple juice, ice cream, cinnamon, nutmeg, and allspice on medium speed for about 1 minute, or until smooth and creamy.

2. Pour into 4 glasses and serve.

TWEENS ON THE SCENE (11+)

This is a super easy recipe, and your tween can make it all on their own. They can even show off their muscles scooping that hard ice cream (see the tip for this on page 14)!

IRELAND WEEK

(ST. PATRICK'S DAY, MARCH 17)

Most St. Patrick's Day festivities involve lots of green and shamrocks and gold coins, but the origin goes all the way back to the fifth century with Saint Patrick bringing Christianity to Ireland. March 17 was the day Saint Patrick passed away. But over time, the holiday has evolved and grown to be not only celebrated in Ireland, but in many countries across the world. Here's how to make Irish Week fun in your home:

- Go green! Have everyone wear their favorite green outfits to give homage to the "Emerald Isle." And while pinching people who don't wear green wasn't a traditional part of St. Patrick's Day, it is a fun practice that the leprechauns would probably approve of.

- In the small town of Cork, Ireland, there is a castle with a famous stone perched on top of the tallest tower—the Blarney Stone. Legend has it that anyone who kisses this stone will have the "Gift of Gab," or the ability to speak eloquently. Take turns having family members try to say some tongue twisters and find out who has the Gift of Gab in your home!

SHE SELLS SEASHELLS BY THE SEASHORE.

PETER PIPER PICKED A PECK OF PICKLED PEPPERS.

FRESH FISH FRY, FRY FRESH FISH.

RED LORRY, YELLOW LORRY, RED LORRY, YELLOW LORRY.

SODA BREAD

MAKES 1 LOAF

4 cups (500 g) all-purpose flour

¾ cup (1½ sticks, or 170 g) butter, softened, divided

⅓ cup (65 g) plus 5 teaspoons granulated sugar, divided

1 tablespoon baking powder

1 teaspoon baking soda

½ teaspoon salt

1 large egg

1½ cups (360 ml) buttermilk, divided

Irish butter, for serving

1. Preheat the oven to 340°F (170°C). Line a half-size baking sheet with parchment paper.

2. In a large bowl, combine the flour, ½ cup (115 g) of the butter, ⅓ cup (65 g) of the sugar, and the baking powder, baking soda, and salt. Mix on low using a hand or stand mixer until combined, about 2 minutes. Add the egg and pour in 1¼ cups (300 ml) of the buttermilk. Mix on low for 2 minutes more until a shaggy dough forms.

3. Change the paddle to a dough hook and knead on low speed (or by hand) for 4 minutes, or until the dough comes together. Wet your hands and remove the dough from the bowl. Form it into a ball and set on the prepared baking sheet. Use a sharp knife to cut a deep X through the middle of the dough, leaving the bottom 1 inch (2.5 cm) intact.

4. Melt the remaining ¼ cup (½ stick, or 55 g) butter, then mix it with the remaining ¼ cup (60 ml) buttermilk. Brush the butter-buttermilk mixture onto the top of the dough and into the X. Sprinkle with 1 teaspoon of the sugar.

5. Bake for 50 minutes, brushing with the butter-buttermilk mixture and sprinkling with 1 teaspoon of the remaining sugar every 10 minutes, or until a knife inserted into the center comes out clean and the top is golden brown. Let cool on a wire rack for 30 minutes before serving with Irish butter.

TWEENS ON THE SCENE (11+)

Show your tween how to carefully remove the bread from the hot oven, then let them take over removing it from the oven, basting it with the butter-buttermilk mixture, sprinkling it with sugar, and returning it to the oven every 10 minutes.

BEEF AND LAMB STEW

SERVES 6

- 1½ pounds (680 g) lamb shoulder, cubed
- 1½ pounds (680 g) beef roast, cubed
- 1 teaspoon salt
- 1 teaspoon ground black pepper
- 3 tablespoons olive oil
- 1 medium yellow onion, diced
- 2 teaspoons minced garlic
- 1 tablespoon tomato paste
- 2 tablespoons all-purpose flour
- 2 cups (480 ml) beef broth
- 1 bay leaf
- 1 sprig fresh rosemary
- 1 teaspoon granulated sugar
- 2 large carrots, peeled and diced
- 2 cups (290 g) quartered baby potatoes
- ⅓ cup (45 g) frozen peas
- ½ cup (120 ml) heavy whipping cream

1. Season the lamb and beef all over with the salt and pepper. In a large pot, heat the oil over medium-high heat. Once glistening, add the lamb and beef. You may need to work in batches. Cook, stirring often, for 5 to 8 minutes, until browned. Transfer to a plate.

2. To the same pot, add the onion, garlic, and 2 tablespoons of water. Cook, while using a wooden spoon to stir and loosen up any browned bits, about 5 minutes, or until the onion is soft. Add the tomato paste and cook for 2 minutes more.

3. Return the lamb and beef to the pot along with the flour. Stir until well combined. Cook, stirring occasionally, for 1 to 2 minutes. Add the beef broth, ¾ cup (180 ml) of water, and the bay leaf, rosemary, and sugar. Stir, cover the pot, and reduce the heat to low. Let cook for 45 minutes.

4. Add the carrots and potatoes and let simmer, uncovered, for an additional 30 to 45 minutes, until the vegetables are fork-tender. Remove and discard the bay leaf and rosemary and add the peas. Cook for 3 minutes, or until the peas are thawed and warmed. Add the cream and stir until well combined.

5. Ladle into soup bowls and serve immediately.

6. Leftovers can be stored in the refrigerator in an airtight container for up to 5 days.

BUDDING SOUS-CHEFS (17+)

The ingredients in this recipe require quite a bit of prep work, so grabbing your older teens to dice and chop ahead of time is great practice for them.

APPLE CAKE

SERVES 8

Nonstick cooking spray

3 cups (375 g) all-purpose flour

2 teaspoons baking powder

¼ teaspoon salt

¼ teaspoon ground cloves

¼ teaspoon ground nutmeg

¾ cup (1½ sticks or 170 g) cold butter, cubed

¾ cup (150 g) plus 1 tablespoon granulated sugar, divided

4 large Granny Smith apples, peeled, cored, and diced

2 large eggs

¾ cup (180 ml) whole milk

Whipped cream or ice cream, for serving

1. Preheat the oven to 375°F (190°C). Grease a 9-inch (23 cm) springform pan with nonstick cooking spray.

2. In a large bowl, stir together the flour, baking powder, salt, cloves, and nutmeg. Drop the cold butter cubes into the mixture and use a pastry cutter or a knife to cut the butter into the mixture. Cut until the butter resembles small pebbles. Stir in ¾ cup (150 g) of the sugar and the apples.

3. In a separate small bowl, beat together the eggs and milk. Pour the egg-milk mixture into the flour mixture and stir well to combine.

4. Pour the dough into the prepared pan and flatten the top with a spatula. Sprinkle the remaining 1 tablespoon sugar over the top. Bake for 45 to 50 minutes, until a toothpick inserted in the center of the cake comes out clean.

5. Serve while still warm with whipped cream or ice cream.

BIG KIDS IN THE KITCHEN (7+)

Cutting the butter into the flour mixture is a pretty safe job (if you keep your fingers out of the bowl!), but may require more arm strength than the littles can muster. Ask your big kid to use their buff arms to work all that cold, hard butter into the flour!

GREECE WEEK

(INDEPENDENCE DAY, MARCH 25)

Opa! Greece is one of the oldest civilizations on earth, and because of that there is a lot of incredible history (and cuisine!) to learn about Greece.

Here are some facts about the recipes in this chapter:

- **TZATZIKI** is a versatile condiment that complements a variety of dishes. From pita bread to salads, its tangy flavor adds a delightful touch. For a tasty twist, use it on all sorts of things, even non-Greek things like fries or sandwiches.

- **SOUVLAKI**, means "skewer" and that's just what it is! Marinated meat and sometimes veggies served straight off the stick or in a warm pita. It's one of the oldest recipes in this cookbook, with some experts tracing it all the way back to 2000 BCE.

- **BAKLAVA,** a beloved treat dating back to the Ottoman Empire, has a rich history that spans centuries. As the Ottoman Empire expanded, baklava's popularity spread, influencing the cuisines of many nations. This cultural exchange has led to the development of countless variations, each with its own unique flavors and textures. Whether you prefer the Greek version or a more innovative twist, baklava's combination of flaky pastry, sweet syrup, and nutty filling is sure to delight your taste buds.

TZATZIKI SAUCE

SERVES 6

1 large cucumber, peeled and grated

1 teaspoon salt

½ teaspoon ground black pepper

2 teaspoons minced garlic

¼ cup (60 ml) olive oil

18 ounces (515 g) plain Greek yogurt

1 tablespoon red wine vinegar

Souvlaki (page 74), for serving (optional)

1. Place the grated cucumber in a medium bowl and sprinkle it with the salt. Let sit for 10 minutes so that the liquid from the cucumber can leach out.

2. Add the cucumbers to a fine-mesh strainer and gently smoosh them with your hands or a wooden spoon to release any excess liquid. Transfer the cucumber to a dry bowl and pat dry with paper towels.

3. Add the pepper, garlic, olive oil, yogurt, and vinegar to the cucumber and stir to combine. Cover and refrigerate for 30 minutes.

4. Drizzle over souvlaki (if using).

5. Leftovers can be kept sealed in the refrigerator up to 1 week.

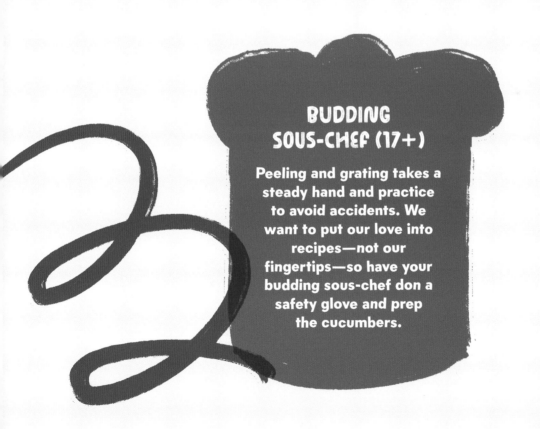

BUDDING SOUS-CHEF (17+)

Peeling and grating takes a steady hand and practice to avoid accidents. We want to put our love into recipes—not our fingertips—so have your budding sous-chef don a safety glove and prep the cucumbers.

SOUVLAKI

MAKES 10 SKEWERS

5 teaspoons minced garlic

2 tablespoons dried oregano

1 teaspoon dried rosemary

1 teaspoon paprika

1 teaspoon salt

1 teaspoon ground black pepper

¼ cup (60 ml) olive oil

½ cup (120 ml) chicken broth

2 tablespoons fresh lemon juice

2½ pounds (1.1 kg) boneless skinless chicken breast, cubed

10 long wooden skewers

Pita bread, for serving (optional)

Chopped tomato, for serving (optional)

Sliced cucumber, for serving (optional)

Tzatziki Sauce (page 73; pictured opposite), for serving (optional)

1. In a food processor or blender, combine the garlic, oregano, rosemary, paprika, salt, pepper, oil, chicken broth, and lemon juice. Pulse until the marinade is creamy, about 1 minute.

2. Place the chicken in a large bowl, pour the marinade over the chicken, and stir to combine. Cover the bowl with plastic wrap and marinate in the refrigerator for at least 1 hour and up to overnight.

3. Soak the wooden skewers in water for at least 30 minutes, so they do not burn when placed on a hot grill grate. Thread the chicken cubes onto the soaked wooden skewers.

4. Preheat a grill or grill pan on the stovetop to medium heat. Place the chicken skewers directly onto the grill grate and cook for about 10 minutes per side, or until the internal temperature reaches 165°F (75°C). Remove from the grill and arrange on a serving plate.

5. Enjoy the chicken on the stick, remove it from the stick and eat it plain, or place it in a pita bread with tomato, cucumber, onions, and tzatziki sauce.

BIG KIDS IN THE KITCHEN (7+)

Using a food processor is safe and fun (if used correctly). Have an adult install the sharp blade into the food processor, then let your Big Kids add the ingredients and push the buttons on the machine.

BAKLAVA

SERVES 20

Nonstick cooking spray

1 cup (100 g) shelled, roasted, salted pecans

1 cup (100 g) walnuts

1 cup (130 g) pistachios

½ cup (70 g) hazelnuts

2 teaspoons ground cinnamon

1 package (16 ounces, or 454 g) fresh or frozen phyllo, thawed

1 cup (2 sticks, or 230 g) salted butter, melted

1 cup (200 g) granulated sugar

1 teaspoon vanilla extract

½ cup (120 ml) honey

TWEENS ON THE SCENE (11+)

Tweens can assemble the entire baklava themselves. Simply model one layer and allow them to complete the rest of the layers.

1. Preheat the oven to 350°F (180°C). Grease a 9 by 13-inch (23 by 33 cm) baking dish with cooking spray.

2. In a food processor or blender, pulse the pecans, walnuts, pistachios, and hazelnuts for about 2 minutes, or until they resemble coarse crumbs. Add the cinnamon and pulse 2 or 3 more times to incorporate.

3. Unroll the phyllo dough and cut it in half widthwise. Set aside 6 half sheets of phyllo for topping at the end. one half sheet of phyllo into the prepared dish and set another sheet on top. Brush with melted butter across the entire surface.

4. Spread 2 to 3 tablespoons of the chopped nuts to cover the dough. Add another 2 half sheets of phyllo, brush with butter, and cover with more nuts. Repeat until your dish is full or you run out of phyllo. Top with the reserved 6 half sheets of phyllo.

5. Use a sharp knife to cut the dough into diamonds by making diagonal cuts across the pan. Bake for 50 to 60 minutes, until the top is golden brown.

6. Meanwhile, bring the sugar and 1 cup (240 ml) of water to a boil over medium-high heat in a small saucepan. Reduce the heat to low, add the vanilla and honey, and let simmer for about 20 minutes, or until slightly thickened. Remove from the heat.

7. Drizzle the syrup over the hot phyllo. Let cool for 5 to 10 minutes before serving.

8. Leave leftovers, uncovered, at room temperature for up to 2 days.

EASTER WEEK

When it comes to celebrating Easter, some people have traditions they adhere to every year and may include the Easter Bunny bringing baskets, Easter egg hunts, ham and potatoes for dinner, or extended family coming to visit. This year, why not try some new traditions? A fun game that is played in many countries around the world (and goes by many names) is Egg Battles. Here is how to play:

1. Hard-boil enough eggs for everyone to have two or three eggs each, and make sure there are no small cracks or fissures in the eggs.

2. Have two contenders stand across from one another, with one person firmly holding one egg above the other person's egg, with both "pointed" ends facing one another.

3. Count "One, Two, Three, HIT" and on "HIT" firmly tap the two eggs together on the pointed ends.

4. Only one of the eggs will crack! See whose egg cracked, and that person needs to flip their egg over and play again with the other side (the "butt" side) of the egg.

5. Keep playing in a bracket style until there is only one person left with an uncracked end of their egg. You can play with multiple eggs per person, or have multiple rounds——whatever you want to do!

CARROT CAKE

SERVES 8

Nonstick cooking spray

3 cups (375 g) all-purpose flour

1 cup (220 g) brown sugar

4 large eggs

1½ cups (300 g) granulated sugar

1 cup (240 ml) vegetable oil

2 teaspoons vanilla extract

1 can (20 ounces, or 567 g) crushed pineapple in pineapple juice, drained

1 tablespoon ground cinnamon

1½ teaspoons baking soda

1 teaspoon salt

4 cups (440 g) grated carrots

1 cup (120 g) chopped walnuts (optional)

1 tub (16 ounces, or 454 g) cream cheese frosting

1. Preheat the oven to 350°F (180°C). Grease two 9-inch (23 cm) round cake pans with nonstick cooking spray.

2. In the bowl of a stand mixer fitted with a paddle attachment, add the flour, brown sugar, eggs, granulated sugar, oil, and vanilla and mix 1 to 2 minutes, until incorporated.

3. Add the pineapple, cinnamon, baking soda, and salt and mix for 1 minute more. Gently stir in the carrots and walnuts (if using) and then divide the batter between the prepared pans.

4. Bake for 45 to 55 minutes, until a toothpick inserted in the center of the cake comes out clean. Let the cakes cool in the pans, about 15 minutes.

5. Run a thin knife around the cake edges to loosen from the side of the pan. Turn the cake, right side up, onto a wire rack to cool completely. Transfer one cake to a cake plate or large plate and spread some cream cheese frosting on the top and sides of the cake. Top with the second cake and spread frosting across the top and down the sides.

BIG KIDS IN THE KITCHEN (7+)

Some kitchen tools make the cooking process more accessible to smaller members of the family. Simply have your big kid add carrot chunks to the top of a rotary grater and press down with the plastic insert while spinning the handle. You'll have grated carrots (and no grated fingers) in no time!

NATURALLY DYED EASTER EGGS

MAKES 6 EGGS

2 tablespoons distilled white vinegar

6 large hard-boiled eggs

Optional Colors

Pink: 2 cups (270 g) shredded red beets

Purple: 2 cups (40 g) loosely packed red onion skins

Blue: 2 cups (190 g) shredded purple cabbage

1. Each of the color options will use 2 tablespoons of vinegar. Multiply the ingredients by the number of colors you would like to make.

2. In a medium saucepan, bring 2 cups (480 ml) of water and 2 cups of your choice of vegetable/color to a boil over medium heat. Once boiling, reduce heat to low and simmer for 30 minutes. Remove from the heat and pour through a sieve into a bowl, discarding solids and reserving the liquid. Add the vinegar to the liquid and stir to combine. Let cool to room temperature, about 45 minutes.

3. Once cooled, add the eggs to the dye, making sure the eggs are completely submerged. Let sit for at least 3 hours and up to overnight in the refrigerator. Remove the eggs from the dye and wipe with a paper towel. Crack and eat or see page 84 for a deviled egg recipe!

LITTLE HELPING HANDS (3+)

Kids love to dye Easter eggs! Once the dyes have cooled, let your little ones dip the eggs into the colors. They can even use white or clear crayons on the eggs first and watch their designs appear after the dye sets!

BIRDS' NESTS

MAKES 12 NESTS

Nonstick cooking spray

1 package (12 ounces, or 340 g) white chocolate chips

1½ cups (360 ml) creamy peanut butter

1 package (12 ounces, or 340 g) crispy chow mein noodles

1 package (10 ounces, or 283 g) package Robin Eggs candy

1. Grease one 12-cup or two 6-cup muffin pans with nonstick cooking spray.

2. In a medium saucepan, melt the white chocolate chips and peanut butter over medium heat.

3. Remove from the heat and stir in the chow mein noodles to coat. While the mixture is still hot, scoop 2 to 3 tablespoons into each muffin-pan cup and press a divot into the center of each nest.

4. Let set for about 20 minutes, then remove the nests from the muffin tin and place several egg candies into each divot.

5. Serve immediately or store at room temperature in an airtight container for up to 4 days.

TWEENS ON THE SCENE (11+)

If you would rather use a microwave instead of the stovetop, your tween can get involved. Place the chocolate chips and peanut butter in a large microwave-safe bowl and microwave on high for 30 seconds, then stir and repeat until the chips just melt. Continue with step 2!

FANCY FOODIE WEEK

While high-quality ingredients can certainly elevate a dish, presentation can play a significant role in determining whether a meal is considered fancy. With a few simple tweaks, even a humble home-cooked meal can be transformed into a gourmet experience. Here are some ideas to elevate your culinary presentations:

- **PLATES.** Most households have a single set of plates. To add a touch of elegance, consider visiting a thrift store or antique shop to acquire unique plates or dishes that catch your eye. There are also groups online called "Buy Nothing" where folks give away things they aren't using for free! Simply search social media for "Buy Nothing (the name of the nearest city or town)."

- **DESIGN.** Instead of simply piling food onto plates, experiment with arranging dishes in visually appealing ways. Try stacking elements in the center and placing the main course on top.

- **AMBIANCE.** A charming tablecloth and a few candles can instantly create a more sophisticated dining atmosphere. For added fun, appoint one of your children as the "waiter" for the evening to enhance the experience.

SHIRLEY TEMPLE

MAKES 4 SHIRLEY TEMPLES

4 cans (7.5 ounces, or 222 ml, each) ginger ale

4 ounces (120 ml) grenadine syrup

Ice

Canned whipped cream

8 maraschino cherries, stems on

1. To a pitcher, add the ginger ale and grenadine and stir to combine.

2. Fill 4 glasses halfway with ice. Divide the ginger ale mixture among the 4 glasses.

3. Top each glass with whipped cream, top with 2 cherries per glass, and serve.

TWEENS ON THE SCENE (11+)

Your tween can make this whole drink! Shirley Temples don't usually have whipped cream, but we are being fancy, so give it a good squirt on top!

DEVILED EGGS

MAKES 12 DEVILED EGGS

6 large eggs

½ cup (120 ml) mayonnaise

1 teaspoon salt

½ teaspoon ground black pepper

¼ teaspoon paprika, plus more for garnishing

Chopped fresh chives, for garnishing (optional)

1. Add the eggs to a medium pot and cover them with cold water. Heat to boiling over high heat. Once boiling, remove the pot from the heat and cover with the lid. Let stand for 15 minutes. Pour out the water, then cover the cooked eggs with cold water to cool them and stop cooking. Once cool, carefully peel the eggs.

2. Slice the eggs in half lengthwise and use a spoon to transfer the yolks to a small bowl. Add the mayonnaise and mash with a fork until smooth and creamy. Stir in the salt, pepper, and paprika.

3. Lay the egg whites on a serving platter, divot sides up. Scoop the filling into a piping bag or zip-top plastic bag with a corner snipped off and squeeze the filling into each egg white half.

4. Garnish with more paprika and chives (if using). Serve immediately.

BIG KIDS IN THE KITCHEN (7+)

Once you have put the filling into the piping bag, ask your big kid to squeeze the filling into each egg. Make sure the bag is snipped with a large enough hole so that the filling doesn't have trouble coming out of the bag.

WHITE CHOCOLATE-COVERED STRAWBERRIES

SERVES 5

1 cup (170 g) white chocolate melting wafers

10 large fresh strawberries, stems on

1. Line a small sheet pan with parchment paper.

2. Place the white chocolate in a small heatproof bowl and microwave for 30 seconds at half power. Stir. Repeat, microwaving and stirring until chocolate just melts.

3. Dip each strawberry completely in the chocolate, leaving the stem clean. Place on the prepared baking sheet and refrigerate for 30 minutes, or until hard. Serve immediately.

LITTLE HELPING HANDS (3+)

Even the little ones can help dip the strawberries! Show them how to scrape off the excess chocolate onto the side of the bowl after each dip—doing so will help prevent a big mess from forming since excess chocolate will pool under the strawberries.

THAILAND WEEK

(SONGKRAN, APRIL 13–15)

We've explored several New Year celebrations throughout this book, and there's still more to come! Thai New Year, known as Songkran, is celebrated in mid-April. Beyond the delicious cuisine, here are some other ways Thais commemorate this festive occasion:

- **WATER SPLASHING.** One of the most exhilarating aspects of Songkran is the water splashing. Imagine a massive water fight taking place throughout the country. People arm themselves with buckets, water guns, and hoses, drenching each other to wash away the misfortunes of the past year.

- **PARADES.** Similar to America's Fourth of July celebrations, Songkran features vibrant parades filled with colorful displays, music, and festive energy.

- **RELIGIOUS CEREMONIES.** Buddhist Thais often visit temples to make offerings to Buddha, such as food, and sprinkle water over Budda statues. This practice is believed to bring good fortune.

PAD THAI

SERVES 4

Noodles

8 ounces (227 g) pad thai rice noodles

Hot water (190°F, or 90°C)

Sauce

3 tablespoons soy sauce

¼ cup (55 g) light brown sugar

2 tablespoons rice vinegar

2 tablespoons creamy peanut butter

Pad Thai

3 tablespoons sesame oil

1 cup (195 g) sliced cooked chicken

1 tablespoon minced garlic

1 medium red bell pepper, thinly sliced

2 large eggs, beaten

3 green onions, sliced

1 cup (90 g) fresh bean sprouts

½ cup (70 g) chopped peanuts

2 limes, quartered

½ cup (20 g) fresh cilantro leaves (optional)

1. To make the noodles: Place the noodles in a large bowl and cover with hot water (see Note). Stir to separate the noodles, then allow to soak for 25 to 30 minutes, until soft. Drain and set aside.

2. To make the sauce: In a small bowl, stir together the soy sauce, brown sugar, rice vinegar, and peanut butter.

3. To make the pad thai: In a large skillet or wok, heat the sesame oil over medium heat. Once shimmering, add the chicken, garlic, and bell pepper and cook until slightly softened, 3 to 4 minutes.

4. Push everything to the side of the pan and pour the egg into the empty side. Cook, stirring often, about 2 minutes, or until set. Stir together everything in the pan. Remove the pan from the heat. Add the noodles, sauce, green onions, and bean sprouts and toss to coat.

5. Pour the pad thai into a serving dish and top with the chopped peanuts, lime wedges, and cilantro (if using).

BUDDING SOUS-CHEFS (17+)

Working with a wok is a hot job, so make sure you keep littles away from the hot pan and utilize your teens to stir the noodles carefully.

NOTE

MOST NOODLES YOU MAKE AT HOME ARE ADDED TO BOILING WATER AND COOKED FOR A CERTAIN AMOUNT OF TIME. THESE NOODLES NEED ONLY TO SOFTEN IN HOT WATER AS THEY ARE MADE OF SOFTER RICE FLOUR RATHER THAN TOUGHER WHEAT FLOUR.

CHICKEN SATAY

MAKES 6 SKEWERS

1 tablespoon creamy peanut butter

½ cup (120 ml) fresh lime juice

¼ cup (60 ml) soy sauce

1 tablespoon brown sugar

1 tablespoon curry powder

1 teaspoon minced garlic

3 boneless, skinless chicken breasts, cubed

6 wooden skewers

1 tablespoon vegetable oil, for greasing grill

Lime wedges, for serving

1. In a medium bowl, stir together the peanut butter, lime juice, soy sauce, brown sugar, curry powder, and garlic. Add the chicken and stir to coat. Cover with plastic wrap and refrigerate 4 to 12 hours to marinate.

2. Soak the wooden skewers in water for at least 30 minutes, so they do not burn when placed on a hot grill grate.

3. Meanwhile, preheat a grill or grill pan on the stovetop to medium heat and grease the grates with vegetable oil (see Tip).

4. Thread the chicken onto the soaked wooden skewers. Place directly on the grill grates and cook for about 5 minutes per side, or until the internal temperature reaches 165°F (75°C).

5. Arrange on a serving platter, or for little ones, remove the meat from the skewers and serve in a large bowl. Serve with lime wedges for squeezing.

TIP

TO EASILY **GREASE** YOUR **GRILL GRATES**, SOAK A PAPER TOWEL IN VEGETABLE OIL. THEN, USE TONGS TO WIPE THE GRILL GRATES WITH THE PREPARED PAPER TOWEL.

TWEENS ON THE SCENE (11+)

Ask your tween if they can check off the items in the ingredient list as you add them to the bowl. Sometimes the most important job is quality control!

MANGO STICKY RICE

SERVES 4

- 1 cup (185 g) glutinous rice (see Note), rinsed
- 1 cup (240 ml) unsweetened coconut milk
- ⅓ cup (65 g) granulated sugar
- ½ teaspoon salt
- 1 can (15 ounces, or 425 g) diced mangos in light syrup, drained
- 1 tablespoon black sesame seeds

1. Prepare the rice according to package instructions or in a rice cooker.

2. Meanwhile, stir together the coconut milk, sugar, and salt over medium heat in a small saucepan for the sauce. Bring to a boil, stirring occasionally. Reduce the heat to low and let simmer for 20 minutes.

3. Once the rice is cooked, transfer it to a large bowl, pour the sauce over the rice, and stir to combine. Cover the bowl with a lid or foil and let the rice soak in the sauce for 15 minutes.

4. Scoop the rice into bowls and top with diced mangos and sprinkle with sesame seeds.

NOTE

GLUTINOUS RICE (ALSO KNOWN AS STICKY RICE) IS A SHORT-GRAIN RICE AVAILABLE AT MOST GROCERY STORES. IT'S ALSO AVAILABLE ONLINE AND AT ASIAN GROCERY STORES. DO NOT SUBSTITUTE OTHER SHORT-GRAIN VARIETIES LIKE ARBORIO.

BIG KIDS IN THE KITCHEN (7+)

Rinsing is an essential part of rice preparation, as it removes excess starches. You can use a special rice strainer to wash and strain the rice, or a normal sieve works well too. Let your big kids add cold water to the rice and swirl to remove the starch, and repeat until the water runs clear.

ITALY WEEK

(LIBERATION DAY, APRIL 25)

April 25 in Italy commemorates Liberation Day, a celebration marking the end of Nazi Germany's occupation during World War II. This joyous occasion is filled with parades, ceremonies, and a sense of national unity.

Italy is renowned for its rich culinary traditions, and visitors often return home inspired to recreate these flavors. Here are some tips for incorporating Italian cuisine into your kitchen:

- **PASTA MACHINE.** Involving children in the kitchen can be fun and educational. Using kitchen appliances, such as pasta machines, simplifies the process by requiring minimal effort. Simply add ingredients to the machine and it does the rest. Pasta machines offer versatility, allowing you to create various shapes and sizes of pasta by changing the extruding tip.

- **HOMEMADE SAUCE.** While store-bought sauces are convenient, making your own sauce at home is simple and allows for customization. Explore your spice cabinet to add unique flavors that reflect your family's preferences, like oregano, parsley, or garlic powder.

ITALIAN-STYLE TOMATO SAUCE

SERVES 6

2 tablespoons olive oil

1 tablespoon minced garlic

¼ cup (13 g) chopped fresh flat-leaf parsley

1 can (28 ounces, 794 g) whole peeled tomatoes

1 tablespoon salt

2 teaspoons dried basil

Fresh basil leaves, for garnish

Pasta, homemade (page 94) or store-bought, for serving

1. In a medium pot, heat the olive oil over medium heat. Once glistening, add the garlic and cook, stirring constantly, until fragrant, about 2 minutes. Add the parsley and cook, stirring constantly, for 2 minutes more.

2. Add the canned tomatoes including juices, salt, and dried basil to the pot and stir to combine. Cover the pot and bring to a boil. Maintain a rapid boil for 5 to 7 minutes. Remove the pot from the heat and let cool for 5 to 10 minutes.

3. Using a blender or an immersion blender, puree the sauce on a low speed until it has reached desired smoothness. Serve over pasta and garnish with fresh basil.

4. Leftovers can be stored in an airtight container in the refrigerator for up to 4 days.

BUDDING SOUS-CHEF (17+)

Immersion blenders are fun little kitchen gadgets but can be tough to master. Show your budding sous-chef how to use it, first away from the boiling hot sauce by practicing on a small bowl of cold water. Once they've shown they can do it carefully, graduate them to the pasta sauce. Make sure everyone in the kitchen wears an apron since the sauce might splash a little.

PASTA MACHINE NOODLES

SERVES 4

1½ cups (190 g) all-purpose flour

5 large egg yolks

1 tablespoon olive oil

2 tablespoons salt

Sauce, homemade (page 93; pictured opposite) or store-bought, for serving

1. Set up a pasta machine with an extruding tip; any tip will do. Have a bowl ready under the extruder to catch the pasta.

2. Fill a large pot with water and bring to a boil over medium heat.

3. Meanwhile, add the flour to the mixing bowl of the pasta machine and shut the lid. Follow the manufacturer instructions to turn the machine on.

4. In a medium bowl, whisk together the egg yolks, 1 tablespoon of water, and the oil. Add the yolk mixture to the pasta machine as it stirs.

5. Once the pasta starts to extrude, use a knife to cut the pasta to the desired length, depending on the pasta type. For penne and rigate, cut 1-inch (2.5 cm) pieces. For spaghetti and linguine, allow them to extrude longer to about 10 inches (25 cm).

6. Add the salt to the boiling water and stir to combine. Add the pasta and cook for 2 to 3 minutes, until the pasta floats to the top of the water. Drain and serve immediately with sauce.

LITTLE HELPING HANDS (3+)

Everyone can help adding ingredients to the pasta machine! Separate the eggs and then have your littles do the whisking (step 4).

BREAD MACHINE ITALIAN BREAD

SERVES 6

1⅓ cups (315 ml) warm water (110°F, or 43°C)

1½ teaspoons olive oil

4 cups (500 g) all-purpose flour, plus more for dusting

1 tablespoon light brown sugar

1½ teaspoons salt

1 package (¼ ounce, or 7 g) active dry yeast

1 large egg

1. In the bowl of a bread machine, add the ingredients in this order, stacking one on top of the other without stirring: the warm water, oil, flour, brown sugar, salt, and yeast. Close the lid, select the "Dough" cycle on the machine, and allow it to run to completion, about 1 hour and 30 minutes; this will mix, knead, and proof the dough, but not bake it.

2. Lightly flour a clean work surface and turn the dough out onto it. Cut the dough into 2 equal portions, then gently knead and shape each piece into a long loaf shape. Cover the dough with a kitchen towel and let rise for 45 minutes.

3. Preheat the oven to 375°F (190°C) and line a baking sheet with parchment paper.

4. Transfer the loaves to the prepared baking sheet.

5. In a small bowl, beat the egg with 1 tablespoon of water. Brush each loaf with the egg wash. Use a sharp knife to cut 3 or 4 diagonal slashes across the top of each loaf.

6. Bake for 30 to 40 minutes, until golden brown and cooked through. Let the loaves cool completely before slicing.

TWEENS ON THE SCENE (11+)

Adding ingredients to the bread machine is fun and easy and doesn't require any stirring on your part! Just explain to your tween that the ingredients go in a certain order and stack just like building blocks.

MEXICO WEEK

(CINCO DE MAYO, MAY 5)

¡Hola! Bienvenido a Mexico Week! Mexico is the United States' neighbor to the south, and until 1848, large parts of the United States were Mexico! Because of our close proximity, lots of Mexican culture is prevalent in the United States including an abundance of Mexican restaurants. Your family is probably familiar with Mexican food already. The following section includes some Mexican recipes that are easy for the family to make together. Here's how to make Mexico Week fun in your home:

"ME GUSTA _____"
(I like _ _ _ _ _)

"¿QUÉ TAL?"
(What's up?)

"¡DE NADA!"
(You're welcome!)

- Open any music streaming service and look up Mexican pop music. Traditional Mexican music has lots of trumpets and accordions—and so does modern Mexican pop music! Play some in the background while you cook.

- How much Spanish do you know? Over 42 million Americans speak Spanish as a first language—and an additional 15 million speak it as a second language—making it the second most spoken language in America after English. Try out a few phrases!

- Browse the Hispanic section at your local grocery store and see if there are any spices or sauces you'd like to include in your Mexican meal. You may find a new favorite seasoning!

OFF-THE-COB MEXICAN ELOTE (CORN)

SERVES 4

1 tablespoon salted butter

2 cans (15.25 ounces, or 432 g, each) sweet corn, drained

2 tablespoons mayonnaise

3 ounces (85 g) finely shredded Monterey Jack cheese

½ teaspoon paprika

1 green onion, sliced

1 tablespoon chopped fresh cilantro

½ teaspoon salt

¼ teaspoon ground black pepper

1 tablespoon fresh lime juice

1 tablespoon Tajín (optional)

1. In a large skillet, melt the butter over medium-high heat. Once bubbling, add the corn and cook, stirring continuously, 10 to 15 minutes, until the kernels are slightly dry and start to char. Remove the pan from the heat and transfer the corn to a large bowl.

2. In a small bowl, stir together the mayonnaise, cheese, paprika, green onion, cilantro, salt, pepper, lime juice, and Tajín (if using).

3. Pour the mayonnaise mixture over the top of the hot corn and stir well to combine.

4. Scoop into a serving bowl or directly onto everyone's plates and serve immediately.

LITTLE HELPING HANDS (3+)

Everyone of any age can help stir up this dish in the final step. Allow little helping hands to sprinkle seasonings into the bowl of corn to their desired spice level—kids are more likely to try new spice flavors if they are the ones to add them!

ENCHILADAS

MAKES 12 ENCHILADAS

Nonstick cooking spray

12 corn tortillas (6 inches, or 15 cm)

1 cup (195 g) cooked, shredded chicken

1 package (10 ounces, or 283 g) queso fresco cheese, crumbled

½ medium white onion, thinly sliced

1 tablespoon dried cilantro

1 teaspoon salt

2 cans (10 ounces, or 283 g, each) mild red enchilada sauce, divided

1 cup (115 g) shredded Monterey Jack cheese

1 avocado, pitted, peeled, and sliced, for serving

BIG KIDS IN THE KITCHEN (7+)

Have an adult cut the avocado in half, then allow big kids to use their thumbs to push the backside of the peel until the pit pops right out. Then, have them use a spoon to scoop out the avocado flesh and a safety knife to slice.

1. Preheat the oven to 375°F (190°C). Grease a 9 by 13-inch (23 by 33 cm) baking dish with nonstick cooking spray.

2. Moisten a paper towel and lay it on a plate. Place the corn tortillas in a stack on the paper towel and place a second moist paper towel over the top of the tortillas. Microwave on high for 45 seconds to soften.

3. In a large bowl, mix the chicken, queso fresco, onion, cilantro, and salt until well combined. Pour half of 1 can of enchilada sauce into the bottom of the prepared baking dish and use a spatula to spread it evenly across the bottom.

4. Place 1 tortilla on a plate or clean surface and scoop ¼ cup (60 g) of filling in a line across the middle of the tortilla. Roll the tortilla closed and place it into the prepared dish, seam side down. Repeat with the remaining tortillas and filling. Top the enchiladas with the remaining 1½ cans enchilada sauce.

5. Bake, uncovered, for 20 minutes. Carefully remove from the oven and sprinkle with the cheese. Return to the oven for 5 minutes more, or until the cheese is melted. Let cool for 10 minutes.

6. Serve topped with avocado slices.

7. Leftovers can be stored in an airtight container in the refrigerator for up to 3 days.

TIP

ENCHILADAS ARE AS **FUN** AS THEY ARE **DELICIOUS**. BECAUSE THEY FOLLOW A BASIC FORMULA, YOU CAN EASILY CUSTOMIZE THEM AS YOU LIKE. SWAP OUT THE CHICKEN FOR ANOTHER PROTEIN, CHANGE UP THE CHEESE, OR EVEN TRY DIFFERENT TORTILLAS OR SAUCES.

KID-FRIENDLY MARGARITAS

MAKES 1 MARGARITA

2 lime wedges, divided

2 tablespoons green sugar sprinkles

1 ½ ounces (45 ml) fresh lime juice (from 2 limes)

3 ounces (90 ml) fresh orange juice

½ ounce (15 ml) agave nectar

2 ounces (60 ml) lemon-lime soda

1. To rim the glass, take a margarita glass (or any glass you like!) and slide 1 of the lime wedges all around the top rim of the glass to moisten it. Pour the green sugar sprinkles into a shallow dish, then turn the cup upside down and place it in the sprinkles. Twist to ensure even coverage. Remove the cup from the sprinkles. Discard any extra sprinkles.

2. To a cocktail shaker, add the lime juice, orange juice, and agave nectar. Fill halfway with ice, close the lid, and shake well.

3. Strain into the prepared glass. Add the lemon-lime soda and fill with ice. Cut a slit into the remaining lime wedge and place it on the rim as a garnish. Serve immediately.

LITTLE HELPING HANDS (3+)

Let your little helper add the sliced limes to the rim of each glass.

TIP

IF YOU'D LIKE TO MAKE THIS FOR A **CROWD**, SIMPLY **MULTIPLY** THE LIME JUICE, ORANGE JUICE, AND AGAVE NECTAR MEASUREMENTS BY HOWEVER MANY PEOPLE YOU ARE SERVING. ADD THEM ALL TO A PITCHER AND **GENTLY STIR** UNTIL COMBINED. THEN, TOP EACH CUP WITH LEMON-LIME SODA.

CHOCOLATE WEEK

Have you ever wondered how chocolate is made? If so, a quick online search will reveal fascinating videos on the process. It all starts with the cacao plant, which produces cacao pods resembling giant nuts. Inside these pods, you'll find a slimy white substance containing tiny beans. These beans must be extracted, dried, and then crushed into a fine powder, which is transformed into a paste. When combined with sugar and milk, this paste becomes the chocolate we know and love. Chocolatiers have perfected this intricate process, turning it into a culinary science.

If you're feeling adventurous, try making your own chocolate from scratch. Begin by purchasing cocoa nibs (which are the crushed, dried beans) from your local grocery store. Use a pestle and mortar to grind the nibs into a paste, then add equal amounts of sugar and milk powder to cocoa nibs to start. Then, add more sugar or milk powder, in small amounts, until you achieve the perfect flavor and texture.

As you'll discover in this chapter, chocolate isn't always sweet. Mole sauce, a savory condiment, is derived from chocolate. Experiment with different ways to incorporate chocolate into your culinary creations.

BROWNIE BITES

MAKES 24 BITES

- ½ cup (1 stick, or 115 g) salted butter, softened
- 1 cup (200 g) granulated sugar
- 2 large eggs
- 1 teaspoon vanilla extract
- ½ cup (50 g) unsweetened cocoa powder
- ½ cup (65 g) all-purpose flour
- ¼ teaspoon salt
- ¼ teaspoon baking powder
- ½ cup (65 g) confectioners' sugar

1. Preheat the oven to 350°F (180°C). Line an 8 by 5-inch (20 x 13 cm) baking dish with parchment paper.

2. In the bowl of a stand mixer fitted with a paddle attachment (or with an electric mixer or by hand), cream the butter, sugar, eggs, and vanilla together. Add the cocoa powder, flour, salt, and baking powder and stir to combine. Scoop the batter into the prepared dish and spread evenly.

3. Bake for 30 minutes, or until a toothpick inserted in the center comes out clean. Let the brownies cool completely in the dish, about 1 hour.

4. Lift the parchment paper up to remove the brownies from the dish. Cut the brownies into 1-inch (2.5 cm) squares.

5. Pour the confectioners' sugar into a paper lunch bag and place 4 brownie squares in the bag. Shake the bag gently to coat the brownies in the sugar. Arrange the brownies on a serving platter and repeat with the remaining brownies.

LITTLE HELPING HANDS (3+)

Let your little helpers shake the bag to coat the brownies with confectioners' sugar. Teach them that if they shake too hard the brownies will break apart, so it takes gentle shaking to create the perfect brownie bites.

CHOCOLATE HUMMUS

SERVES 6

1 can (15.5 ounces, or 439 g) chickpeas, rinsed and drained

⅓ cup (79 g) tahini

¼ cup (25 g) unsweetened cocoa powder

¼ cup (60 ml) maple syrup

2 tablespoons agave nectar

1 teaspoon vanilla extract

½ teaspoon salt

Chopped walnuts, for garnishing (optional)

Optional Dippers

Graham crackers

Marshmallows

Cookies

Pretzels

Fruit

Vegetables

1. Add the chickpeas, tahini, cocoa powder, maple syrup, agave, vanilla, and salt to a food processor or blender and process for 1 to 2 minutes, until smooth.

2. Scoop the hummus into a bowl, garnish with walnuts (if using), and serve with dippers.

LITTLE HELPING HANDS (3+)

Little kids love pressing buttons! Add all the ingredients to the food processor and let your little helper push the "On" button. Usually food processors and blenders have a "pulse" function that your little ones can smash many times in a row to create the perfect hummus texture.

MOLE SAUCE

SERVES 4

2 tablespoons olive oil

½ cup (55 g) chopped onion

2 tablespoons minced garlic

1 teaspoon dried oregano

1 teaspoon ground cumin

¼ teaspoon ground cinnamon

1 teaspoon chili powder

2 tablespoons all-purpose flour

2 cups (480 ml) chicken broth

2 tablespoons dark chocolate chips

Grilled chicken or Enchiladas (page 100), for serving

1. In a large saucepan, heat the oil over low heat until shimmering. Add the onion and garlic and cook, stirring frequently, 8 to 10 minutes, until softened. Add the oregano, cumin, cinnamon, chili powder, and flour and stir to combine and cook for 3 minutes more.

2. Slowly whisk in the chicken broth, increase the heat to medium-high, and bring the mixture to a boil. Reduce the heat to low and let simmer, uncovered, for 30 minutes. Remove from the heat and whisk in the chocolate; whisk until the chocolate is melted and evenly distributed in the sauce.

3. Serve over grilled chicken or on enchiladas.

TWEENS ON THE SCENE (11+)

If you have a box chopper, you can involve your tween in the prep process. A box chopper allows you to create perfectly identical cuts every time and is much safer than using a knife. You simply set the food to be cut inside and then shut the lid. Be sure to supervise!

EGYPT WEEK

(EID AL-ADHA)

RECIPES

Eid al-Adha, or the Feast of Sacrifice, is a significant Islamic holiday celebrated in the twelfth month of the Islamic calendar. It commemorates Prophet Ibrahim's (Abraham) willingness to sacrifice his son as an act of obedience to God. During this time, Muslim families gather to pray, exchange gifts, and share festive meals.

Egypt, with its rich history dating back to the era of the pharaohs and the pyramids, holds a special place in the world's cultural heritage. The ancient Egyptians practiced mummification, believing in an afterlife. Their hieroglyphics, intricate symbols carved into walls and artifacts, have provided invaluable insights into their civilization.

For a fun family activity, try building the tallest pyramid you can with sugar cubes. Remember, a wider base is crucial for a taller structure!

SAHLAB

MAKES 4 SAHLABS

4 cups (960 ml) whole milk

3½ tablespoons cornstarch

2 tablespoons granulated sugar

1 teaspoon vanilla extract

1 teaspoon ground cinnamon

1 tablespoon shredded coconut

¼ cup (30 g) chopped
  pistachios

2 tablespoons golden raisins

1. In a small saucepan, heat the milk, cornstarch, sugar, and vanilla over medium heat, whisk until the mixture comes to a boil, then keep boiling for 2 minutes.

2. Remove the pan from the heat and pour the mixture evenly into 4 mugs.

3. Sprinkle with the cinnamon, coconut, pistachios, and raisins. Serve warm.

BIG KIDS IN THE KITCHEN (7+)

Your big kid can help set out the toppings for the drink, and even choose which ones you want to buy from the store. If there are toppings your big kid likes better (like maybe peanuts, chocolate chips, or sprinkles) offer those as options too!

QAMAR AL-DIN

MAKES 4 DRINKS

1 cup (160 g) dried apricots
¼ cup (50 g) granulated sugar

1. In a small saucepan, bring 3 cups (720 ml) of water and the apricots to a boil over medium heat. Reduce the heat to low and let simmer for 15 to 20 minutes, until the apricots are soft. Let the mixture cool in the pan for 5 to 10 minutes.

2. Pour the entire contents of the pan into a blender (or use an immersion blender) and add the sugar. Blend on medium for about 2 minutes, or until smooth.

3. Cover and place in the refrigerator to cool completely, about 1 hour.

4. Pour into 4 glasses over ice and serve immediately.

BUDDING SOUS-CHEFS (17+)

Working with hot liquid can be tricky, but your sous-chef can handle it! Have your sous-chef be extra careful when pouring so she does not burn herself.

KOFTA

MAKES 8 KOFTAS

1 pound (454 g) ground beef

1 cup (110 g) diced white onion

½ cup (25 g) chopped fresh flat-leaf parsley

2 teaspoons minced garlic

1 tablespoon ground cumin

1 teaspoon ground coriander

½ teaspoon ground paprika

½ teaspoon salt

¼ teaspoon ground black pepper

¼ cup (25 g) plain dried bread crumbs

1 large egg, beaten

Optional Sandwich Fixings

Pita bread

Vegetables (such as shredded lettuce, sliced tomato, sliced onion)

Sauce (such as Tzatziki on page 73, hummus, or yogurt-tahini)

1. In a large bowl, mix the ground beef, onion, parsley, garlic, cumin, coriander, paprika, salt, pepper, bread crumbs, and egg until well combined.

2. Divide the meat mixture into 8 equal portions, form each portion into an elongated oval, and set on a plate.

3. Heat a large skillet over medium heat. Add the meat ovals to the pan and cook 15 to 20 minutes, then flip and cook for an additional 15 to 20 minutes, until the beef is cooked through and reaches an internal temperature of 160°F (70°C) and the outsides are browned.

4. Serve alone or as sandwiches in pita bread with veggies and sauce.

BIG KIDS IN THE KITCHEN (7+)

Get some gloves on your big kid and let them mix and squish the meat mixture until everything is all combined. It is going to feel weird at first, but they will probably like the idea of playing with their food!

NEW ENGLAND WEEK

New England encompasses the states of Maine, New Hampshire, Vermont, Massachusetts, Rhode Island, and Connecticut. While each state possesses its unique identity, New England as a region is renowned for its breathtaking fall foliage and historic towns. It is also home to some stunning coastal landscapes. This week, enjoy some of the charm of region, which boasts a distinctive culinary heritage shaped by the region's abundant flora and fauna.

Lobster fishing is a cornerstone of New England's economy, with fishermen harvesting lobsters that are shipped worldwide. If you ever visit the region, don't miss the opportunity to savor freshly caught lobster. In the meantime, the lobster you enjoy at your local grocery store may have originated from the shores of New England.

Clams are another abundant marine resource in New England, contributing to the iconic dish of clam chowder. Harvesters use a dredge, a large metal basket, to gather clams from the ocean floor, which are then sorted and cleaned.

BOSTON BAKED BEANS

SERVES 6

2 cans (15 ounces, or 425 g) navy beans, rinsed and drained, divided

6 slices thick-cut bacon, divided

½ medium yellow onion, diced, divided

½ cup (120 ml) ketchup

¼ cup (55 g) brown sugar

3 tablespoons molasses

1 tablespoon Worcestershire sauce

2 teaspoons salt

½ teaspoon ground black pepper

2 teaspoons ground mustard

1. Preheat the oven to 325°F (170°C).

2. Add 1 can of the beans to a 9 by 13-inch (23 by 33 cm) dish and lay 3 of the bacon slices on top of the beans, followed by half of the diced onion. Repeat with the remaining can of beans, 3 slices of bacon, and diced onion.

3. In a medium saucepan, combine the ketchup, brown sugar, molasses, Worcestershire sauce, salt, pepper, and ground mustard over medium heat. Bring to a boil and then remove the saucepan from the heat.

4. Pour the mixture over the beans, cover with foil, and bake for 3 hours and 30 minutes, stirring every 30 minutes. Remove from the oven and serve.

BUDDING SOUS-CHEFS (17+)

Making baked beans is kind of like building a lasagna—putting layers on top of one another in a dish. The layering isn't hard, but pouring the boiling sauce over the layers can be tricky. Make sure your budding sous-chef is wearing heat-resistant mitts when handling the hot pot.

LOBSTER ROLLS

SERVES 4

¼ cup (½ stick, or 55 g) salted butter, softened

4 split-top hoagie or hot dog buns

1 pound (454 g) cooked lobster meat, cut into chunks

3 tablespoons fresh lemon juice

½ teaspoon salt

½ teaspoon lemon pepper

¼ cup (25 g) chopped celery

⅓ cup (75 ml) mayonnaise

1. Spread the butter on the outsides of each bun. In a large skillet, toast the buns, butter sides down, over medium-high heat until golden.

2. In a medium bowl, stir together the lobster, lemon juice, salt, lemon pepper, celery, and mayonnaise.

3. Scoop the lobster filling into the toasted buns and serve.

BIG KIDS IN THE KITCHEN (7+)

Instead of scooping the mayo out of a jar, consider buying a squeeze bottle of mayo and letting your big kids squeeze the mayo directly into the lobster mix. It is okay to eyeball the amount for this recipe—just start with less and add more as needed.

CLAM CHOWDER

SERVES 8

½ cup (1 stick, or 115 g) salted butter

½ cup (65 g) all-purpose flour

2 tablespoons vegetable oil

2 large yellow potatoes, peeled and diced

1 medium white onion, diced

2 medium ribs celery, diced

1½ cups (360 ml) heavy whipping cream

1 cup (240 ml) clam juice

2 cans (6.5 ounces, or 184 g, each) chopped clams in juice

1 teaspoon ground thyme

½ teaspoon salt

½ teaspoon ground black pepper

Bacon bits, for garnishing

1. In a small saucepan, melt the butter over medium heat. Sprinkle in the flour and cook, whisking continuously, until golden brown, about 5 minutes. Remove the pan from the heat.

2. In a large saucepan, heat the oil over medium heat. Add the potatoes, onion, and celery and cook for 10 minutes, or until the onion is softened.

3. Add the cream, clam juice, clams and their juices, thyme, salt, and pepper. Add the butter-flour mixture and stir to combine. Bring to a boil over medium heat, then reduce the heat to low and let simmer for 5 minutes, or until the potatoes are soft.

4. Ladle the chowder into bowls, sprinkle with bacon bits, and serve.

BIG KIDS IN THE KITCHEN (7+)

This soup is delicious on its own but can be enhanced by some yummy toppings. Have your big kid choose and set out their favorite soup toppings. This might include bacon bits, oyster crackers, sour cream, or anything else they can dream up!

PICNIC WEEK

Grab your comfiest blanket and prepare for a delightful picnic! While any food can be enjoyed as a picnic, the following chapter highlights classic picnic fare that travels well.

The iconic wicker picnic basket, often featuring straps to secure plates, cups, and cutlery, is definitely cute and fun, but not everyone owns one of these. A reusable grocery bag can serve just as well. Dedicate a specific bag for picnics to excite your family whenever they see it.

Explore different picnic locations and discover your family's favorite spots. Remember, picnics aren't exclusively outdoor events. Laying a blanket on your living room floor can create a festive and enjoyable atmosphere.

MAGIC COOKIE BARS

SERVES 12

9 graham crackers

½ cup (1 stick, or 115 g) salted butter, melted

¾ cup (130 g) semisweet chocolate chips

¾ cup (130 g) butterscotch chips

¾ cup (65 g) sweetened shredded coconut

¾ cup (90 g) chopped pecans

1 can (14 ounces, or 396 g) sweetened condensed milk

1. Preheat the oven to 350°F (180°C). Line a 9 by 13-inch (23 by 33 cm) baking dish with parchment paper.

2. In the bowl of a food processor or blender, add the graham crackers and pulse until crumbly. Add the melted butter and pulse a few more times to incorporate. Scrape the mixture into the prepared baking dish and press into the bottom of the pan using a spatula.

3. Sprinkle the chocolate chips, butterscotch chips, coconut, and pecans across the entire surface of the graham crackers. Drizzle the sweetened condensed milk over everything.

4. Bake for 30 minutes, or until the edges are brown and everything is melty. Let the bars cool completely before cutting, then wrap individually in wax paper to pack for your picnic.

BIG KIDS IN THE KITCHEN (7+)

You know something magic about these bars? You can customize them as you like! Bring your big kid to the baking or cookie aisle of the grocery store and see what they would like in their magic bars. Some ideas: crushed cookies, dried cranberries, raisins, or sprinkles!

TURKEY BLT PINWHEELS

MAKES 16 PINWHEELS

2 flour tortillas (10 inches, or 25 cm)

¼ cup (60 g) cream cheese, softened

4 slices cooked bacon

8 slices turkey lunch meat

6 slices provolone cheese

4 pieces iceberg or romaine lettuce

1. Lay both tortillas on a clean countertop and spread the entire surface of each with the cream cheese. Onto each wrap, lay the bacon slices across the middle, followed by the turkey, provolone, and lettuce.

2. Starting with the edge closest to you, roll the wrap into a tight jell roll.

3. Wrap each roll in plastic wrap and refrigerate for 20 minutes.

4. Remove the rolls from the refrigerator and slice each roll through the plastic wrap into 8 pinwheels. Remove the plastic wrap and lay the pinwheels, flat sides down, in a lunch box to take on your picnic.

TWEENS ON THE SCENE (11+)

Ask your tween to spread the softened cream cheese onto the wraps using a butter knife or spatula. If you need to soften the cream cheese in a jiffy, simply remove any packaging, place in a heatproof bowl, and microwave for 30 seconds on 50 percent power. Repeat until soft.

PICKLE PASTA SALAD

SERVES 6

½ cup (120 ml) mayonnaise

½ cup (120 ml) sour cream

½ cup (120 ml) dill pickle juice

1 packet (1 ounce, or 28 g) ranch seasoning

1 cup (145 g) chopped dill pickles

½ cup (40 g) bacon bits

2 tablespoons chopped fresh dill

1 block (8 ounces, or 227 g) cheddar cheese, cubed

16 ounces (454 g) cooked, drained, and cooled ditalini pasta (see Note)

NOTE

THESE ADORABLE LITTLE PASTA TUBES SOAK UP EVERY BIT OF FLAVOR, BUT IF YOU CAN'T FIND DITALINI, FARFALLE (BOW TIE) PASTA IS A GREAT ALTERNATIVE.

1. In a large bowl, whisk together the mayonnaise, sour cream, dill pickle juice, and ranch seasoning until smooth. Stir in the pickles, bacon bits, dill, and cheese.

2. Add the cooked pasta and fold it in until well coated.

3. Cover the pasta salad and chill for 30 minutes.

4. Scoop into 6 individual containers with lids for your picnic.

BUDDING SOUS-CHEFS (17+)

Ask your budding sous-chef if they would like to take the reins on and cook all the items for the picnic. They could also pack up the food and other picnic supplies such as utensils and napkins. You could even have them choose the day and location for your picnic.

UNITED KINGDOM WEEK

The United Kingdom comprises England, Scotland, Wales, and Northern Ireland, each with its own distinct culinary traditions. For this chapter, we'll explore the diverse flavors of the United Kingdom as a whole.

While the United Kingdom is often stereotyped as having bland cuisine, this misconception is far from the truth. The country offers a variety of delicious dishes that showcase its rich culinary heritage. The following recipes capture a glimpse of the food found across the United Kingdom, including the iconic Yorkshire pudding (not a dessert like vanilla or chocolate pudding!), buttery scones, and the sweet Eton Mess.

If you're from the United States, the United Kingdom is a highly accessible travel destination, with flights from New York to London taking just a few hours. As English is the native language, communication is relatively straightforward for English speakers. International travel isn't in the cards for every family, but no bother, these recipes are here for you to take an imaginary trip to the UK any time you like! So, cheerio and enjoy United Kingdom Week!

YORKSHIRE PUDDING

MAKES 12 PUDDINGS

3 tablespoons butter, cut into 12 cubes

3 large eggs

1 cup (240 ml) whole milk

1 cup (125 g) all-purpose flour

Hearty stew, for serving (optional)

1. Place one cube of butter into each cup of one 12-cup or two 6-cup muffin pans. Place the pan(s) in the oven while it preheats to 375°F (190°C).

2. In a medium bowl, whisk together the eggs, milk, and flour. Once the oven has reached the set temperature, carefully remove the muffin pan(s) and evenly divide the batter into the buttered cups.

3. Bake for 5 minutes, then reduce the oven temperature to 350°F (180°C) and bake for 25 minutes more, or until puffy and browned.

4. Remove from the oven and serve warm with a hearty stew (if using).

LITTLE HELPING HANDS (3+)

It is important not to open the oven at any time during the baking process, or else the puddings will deflate. Let your little helper know they need to stand guard and not let anyone open the oven until the puddings are done!

SCONES

MAKES 12 SCONES

2 cups (250 g) all-purpose flour, plus more for dusting

3 tablespoons granulated sugar

2 tablespoons baking powder

½ teaspoon salt

3 tablespoons cold salted butter, cut into small cubes

¾ cup (180 ml) whole milk

1 large egg yolk

1 tablespoon heavy whipping cream

Butter, for serving

Jam, for serving

1. Preheat the oven to 425°F (220°C). Line a baking sheet with parchment paper.

2. In the bowl of a food processor fitted with the blade attachment, add the flour, sugar, baking powder, and salt. While pulsing, add the butter one cube at a time until all the butter is added; the mixture should be crumbly. Continue to pulse as you slowly pour in the milk and the dough comes together into a rough ball.

3. Lightly flour a clean work surface. Transfer the dough to it and knead for 2 minutes. Using a lightly floured rolling pin, roll the dough out to about 1 inch (2.5 cm) thick.

4. Use a 2- to 3-inch (5 to 7.5 cm) round biscuit cutter or the lip of a thin glass to cut the dough into circles (see Tip). Cut out about 12 rounds (you can smoosh together any remaining dough pieces and re-roll to cut more rounds). Place the rounds 1 inch (2.5 cm) apart on the prepared baking sheet.

5. In a small bowl, whisk together the egg yolk and cream. Brush the tops of the scones with the egg wash.

6. Bake for 12 to 15 minutes, until golden brown. Let cool completely on the pan, about 45 minutes,

7. Serve with butter and jam.

TIP

FOR THE **BEST RESULTS**, FLOUR THE BISCUIT CUTTER OR GLASS, THEN PUSH STRAIGHT DOWN AND PULL UP WITHOUT TWISTING.

BIG KIDS IN THE KITCHEN (7+)

Using a biscuit cutter is just like using tools while playing with Play-Doh! Work together and help your big kids push straight down and pull straight up.

ETON MESS

SERVES 6

24 miniature vanilla meringue
cookies, divided

1½ pounds (680 g) strawberries,
hulled and quartered, divided

Zest and juice of 1 lime

¼ cup (30 g) confectioners'
sugar

2 cups (480 ml) heavy whipping
cream

1. Add 12 of the meringue cookies to a zip-top plastic bag. Gently crush the cookies using a rolling pin.

2. In a medium bowl, place ½ pound (227 g) of the strawberries and mash with a fork until a smooth puree forms. Add the lime zest and juice and stir to combine. Stir in the remaining 1 pound (454 g) of strawberries.

3. In a large bowl, using a hand or stand mixer, whisk the confectioners' sugar and whipping cream for about 3 to 5 minutes, until stiff peaks form. Use a spatula to fold in the crushed meringue cookies.

4. Divide the strawberry mixture and whipped cream mixture among 6 clear, tall parfait glasses, taking care to alternate between layers of strawberry and whipped cream, finishing with a whipped cream layer. Top with 2 of the remaining meringue cookies per cup. Serve immediately.

BIG KIDS IN THE KITCHEN (7+)

Using a masher requires some big muscles, so you'd better call your big kid to come help you manage it!

SUMMER SALAD WEEK

Salads are a refreshing and healthy option any time of year, but they're particularly enjoyable during the summer when you want to avoid heating up your home with the oven or stove. Plus, they can be packed with fresh, seasonal produce.

Have you explored your local farmers market? These markets often take place on weekends and feature local farmers, bakers, and artisans selling their fresh produce and handcrafted goods. In addition to fresh produce, you'll likely find preserved items like salsa, salad dressings, and pasta sauces. Make it a point to visit your local farmers market regularly, as the changing seasons bring a variety of new products throughout the year.

As you'll discover in this chapter, salads can be incredibly versatile and are limited only by your imagination. Simply combine various ingredients, drizzle with a dressing of your choice, and voilà! You have a delicious salad.

TACO SALAD

SERVES 6

Taco-Seasoned Beef

1 teaspoon chili powder

½ teaspoon salt

½ teaspoon pepper

¼ teaspoon garlic powder

¼ teaspoon onion powder

¼ teaspoon smoked paprika

¼ teaspoon dried oregano

¼ teaspoon ground cumin

½ pound (227 g) ground beef

Salad

1 bag (8 ounces, or 227 g) shredded iceberg lettuce

1 cup (260 g) canned black beans, rinsed and drained

1 cup (165 g) canned sweet corn, drained

1 cup (145 g) cherry tomatoes, halved

1 large avocado, pitted, peeled, and cubed

½ cup (120 ml) sour cream

½ cup (55 g) shredded cheddar cheese

½ cup (120 ml) favorite salsa

Tortilla chips (about 10 chips per serving)

Chopped fresh cilantro, for garnishing (optional)

1. **To make the taco-seasoned beef:** In small bowl, mix the chili powder, salt, pepper, garlic powder, onion powder, smoked paprika, oregano, and cumin until well combined for the taco seasoning.

2. In a large skillet over medium heat, cook the beef, while breaking it up with a wooden spoon, for 7 to 10 minutes, until browned and cooked through.

3. Add the taco seasoning and stir to coat the beef. Remove the skillet from the heat and let the meat cool for 5 minutes.

4. **To make the salad:** In a large serving bowl, toss together the taco-seasoned ground beef, lettuce, black beans, corn, tomatoes, avocado, sour cream, cheddar cheese, and salsa. Sprinkle with the crushed tortilla chips, garnish with cilantro (if using), and serve.

TWEENS ON THE SCENE (11+)

Have you ever seen a grape cutter? This little kitchen tool halves or quarters a grape in one click. This tool is also great for cutting cherry tomatoes! Teach your tween how to use it and have them chop the tomatoes while you work on the rest of the salad.

CHOPPED SALAD

SERVES 6

1 bag (9 ounces, or 255 g) chopped romaine lettuce mix

1 cup (165 g) canned sweet corn, drained

1 cup (145 g) cherry tomatoes, halved

1 cup (145 g) diced cucumbers

1 large avocado, peeled, pitted, and diced

½ cup (40 g) bacon bits

1 cup (195 g) bite-size pieces cooked chicken breast

¼ cup (60 ml) ranch dressing

In a large serving bowl, toss together the lettuce, corn, tomatoes, cucumbers, avocado, bacon bits, chicken, and ranch until evenly coated. Serve immediately.

TIP

A **FUN** way to **MIX** your salad is to load all the **INGREDIENTS** into a large plastic container and secure the lid tightly. Ask a helper to **SHAKE** the container vigorously to **EVENLY COAT** the salad and disperse the ingredients.

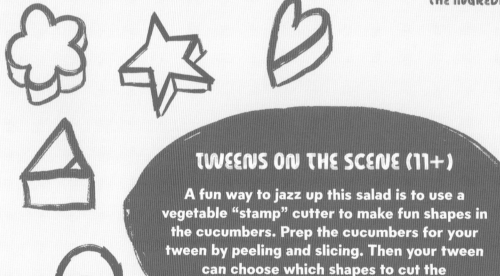

TWEENS ON THE SCENE (11+)

A fun way to jazz up this salad is to use a vegetable "stamp" cutter to make fun shapes in the cucumbers. Prep the cucumbers for your tween by peeling and slicing. Then your tween can choose which shapes to cut the cucumbers into. Optional, but cute!

FRUIT SALAD

SERVES 6

1 cup (165 g) hulled and chopped strawberries

1 cup (175 g) peeled and chopped kiwi

1 cup (165 g) peeled, pitted, and chopped mango

1 cup (160 g) peeled, seeded, and cubed cantaloupe

1 cup (133 g) peeled and diced cucumber

1 cup (145 g) seeded and diced orange bell pepper

¼ cup (60 ml) poppyseed dressing

In a large bowl, toss together the strawberries, kiwi, mango, cantaloupe, cucumber, bell pepper, and dressing until evenly coated. Serve immediately.

BIG KIDS IN THE KITCHEN (7+)

Allow your big kid to help you choose ingredients for your fruit salad. These ingredients are just suggestions. Any fruit will do! Grapes, apples, pears, and raspberries are all great options. Visit a local farmers market and fill your salad with in-season produce grown by your neighbors!

HAWAII WEEK

(KING KAMEHAMEHA DAY, JUNE 11)

Aloha and welcome to the Islands! Hawaii is an incredible place with a variety of influences by cultures who settled the little chain of islands in the Pacific throughout time—and their food displays that fusion. Here are some ways to make Hawaii Week fun in your home:

- Stop by a local party store to grab some leis for everyone to wear. Leis are necklaces made from flowers (fresh or artificial) given as a greeting of warmth and love. Party stores might also have other Hawaiian-inspired items, such as grass skirts or coconut drinking cups.

- Watch a YouTube video on how to do a simple hula dance. Everyone will have a great time learning together! It's okay if you feel silly at first, just lean into it and enjoy the moment.

- Learn a few words in Hawaiian to speak to one another:

"ALOHA"
(ah-LO-ha):
hello *and*
goodbye

A HUI HOU
(ah-hoo-wee HOO):
until we meet again

"MAHALO"
(ma-HA-lo):
thank you

MACARONI SALAD

SERVES 6

1 box (16 ounces, or 454 g) elbow pasta

1 tablespoon granulated sugar

1 tablespoon apple cider vinegar

3 cups (720 ml) mayonnaise, divided

½ cup (65 g) finely minced onion, rinsed (to remove bitterness)

½ cup (55 g) shredded carrots

½ teaspoon white pepper

1. Bring a large pot of water to a boil over medium-high heat. Add the noodles and cook for 12 minutes, or until soft (beyond al dente). Drain and transfer to a large bowl.

2. Stir the sugar, vinegar, and 1 cup (240 ml) of the mayonnaise into the pasta. Refrigerate for 20 minutes.

3. Stir the remaining 2 cups (480 ml) mayonnaise, the onion, carrots, and white pepper into the pasta. Refrigerate for at least 1 hour or up to overnight, before serving.

4. Leftovers can be covered and refrigerated for up to 4 days.

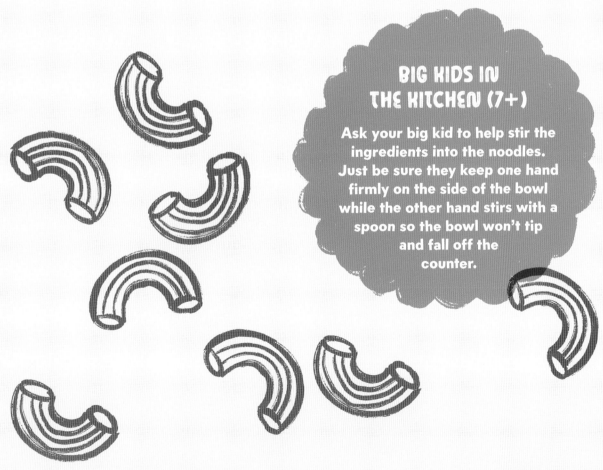

BIG KIDS IN THE KITCHEN (7+)

Ask your big kid to help stir the ingredients into the noodles. Just be sure they keep one hand firmly on the side of the bowl while the other hand stirs with a spoon so the bowl won't tip and fall off the counter.

TERIYAKI CHICKEN THIGHS

MAKES 12 CHICKEN THIGHS

2 cups (480 ml) soy sauce

2 cups (480 ml) pineapple juice

2 cups (440 g) light brown sugar

3 tablespoons minced garlic

2 tablespoons minced fresh ginger

3 pounds (1.4 kg) boneless, skinless chicken thighs, fat trimmed

Sliced green onions, for garnishing (optional)

Sesame seeds, for garnishing (optional)

Rice, for serving (optional)

1. In a large bowl, stir together the soy sauce, pineapple juice, brown sugar, garlic, and ginger. Add the chicken and toss to coat. Cover the bowl with plastic wrap, then refrigerate overnight or up to 3 days, stirring occasionally.

2. Preheat a grill to medium-high or set a grill pan over medium-high heat.

3. Use tongs to transfer the chicken thighs from the marinade to the grill. Discard the excess marinade. Grill the chicken for 8 to 10 minutes per side, until the internal temperature reaches 165°F (75°C).

4. Transfer the chicken to a serving platter, garnish with the green onions (if using) and/or sesame seeds (if using), and serve with rice (if using).

5. Leftover chicken can be stored in an airtight container in the refrigerator for up to 4 days.

LITTLE HELPING HANDS (AGE 3+)

Allow small children to help stir the ingredients together in the large bowl, while teaching them about bacteria that can exist on raw chicken. Safety in the kitchen includes washing hands thoroughly and keeping surfaces and utensils clean!

SPAM MUSUBI

MAKES 12 MUSUBI

2 cups (330 g) cooked white rice

2 tablespoons rice vinegar

1 tablespoon mirin (Japanese rice wine)

½ cup (100 g) granulated sugar

¼ cup (60 ml) soy sauce

¼ cup (60 ml) oyster sauce

1 can (12 ounces, or 340 g) Spam, cut into 8 slices

2 tablespoons vegetable oil

3 sheets (7 by 8 inches, or 18 by 20 cm) nori (dried seaweed)

1. In a large bowl, stir together the rice, rice vinegar, and mirin.

2. In a shallow dish, stir together the sugar, soy sauce, and oyster sauce for a marinade. Place the Spam slices in the marinade and let sit for 10 minutes.

3. In a large nonstick skillet, heat the oil over medium heat. Add the marinated Spam and cook for about 3 minutes per side, or until lightly browned. Transfer to a plate.

4. Slice the nori sheets lengthwise into thirds. Lay 1 strip of nori on a clean surface or plate and scoop ¼ cup (60 g) rice mixture onto the center, using wet hands to form into a rectangle the same size as a slice of Spam. Carefully place 1 slice of cooked Spam on top of the rice, then bring up the ends of the nori strip and overlap them over the top of the Spam and rice, using a wet finger to moisten and seal the end.

5. Repeat step 4 with the remaining ingredients (eat or discard the remaining strip of nori). Serve immediately.

TWEENS ON THE SCENE (11+)

There are a lot of ways to prepare rice: You can cook it from raw rice grains in a pot on the stove or in a rice cooker, or you can buy instant dried rice that can be cooked up in a few minutes, or even little cups of precooked rice that just need a minute in the microwave. Use whatever your family prefers and has time for!

NIGERIA WEEK

(DEMOCRACY DAY, JUNE 12)

June 12 marks Democracy Day in Nigeria, commemorating the annulment of the 1993 presidential election, a controversial event that sparked widespread outrage and unrest. In 1999, Nigeria declared June 12 as Democracy Day to honor those who fought for fair elections.

Trying a new cuisine can be a fun and rewarding experience. To celebrate Nigeria, consider preparing the dishes featured in this chapter. You'll find recipes for:

- **JOLLOF.** A popular rice dish teeming with savory flavors.

- **FUFU.** A tasty side dish made from plantains that can be used to scoop up bites of your main dish.

- **CHIN CHIN.** Tiny cookie-like bites perfect for a sweet treat.

For a visual exploration of Nigerian culture, search online for "Nigerian colorful patterns." You'll be amazed by the vibrant and intricate designs incorporated into their textiles. Gather some construction paper and challenge your family to create your own colorful patterns.

JOLLOF

SERVES 6

2 tablespoons vegetable oil

1 medium yellow onion, diced

2 tablespoons minced garlic

1 teaspoon minced fresh ginger

1 cup (185 g) uncooked long-grain rice

1½ cups (360 ml) chicken stock

1 can (15 ounces, or 430 g) crushed tomatoes

1 teaspoon salt

½ teaspoon curry powder

½ teaspoon dried thyme

½ teaspoon paprika

1 bay leaf

Fresh thyme, for garnishing (optional)

Fufu (page 140; pictured opposite), for serving (optional)

1. In a large pot, heat the oil over medium heat. Once glistening, add the onion and cook, stirring often, for about 5 minutes, or until soft. Add the garlic and ginger and cook 1 minute more.

2. Stir in the rice and continue to stir for 2 minutes, or until the rice is toasted. Add the chicken stock, tomatoes, salt, curry powder, dried thyme, paprika, and bay leaf and bring to a boil.

3. Reduce the heat to low and let simmer for 30 minutes, or until the liquid is evaporated and the rice is cooked. Turn off the heat, cover, and let rest 10 minutes to finish cooking.

4. Remove the bay leaf, garnish with fresh thyme (if using), and serve with fufu (if using).

BUDDING SOUS-CHEFS (17+)

This dish is a bit tougher for smaller kids, but your budding sous-chef can handle it no problem. It mostly just cooks itself! Have your sous-chef make this whole dish from start to finish, with you nearby, ready to lend a hand if they need it.

FUFU

MAKES 6 FUFU

3 ripe plantains, peeled and cut into chunks

Jollof (page 138), for serving (optional)

1. In a blender or food processor, process the plantains and 1 cup (240 ml) of water on medium-low speed for about 2 minutes, or until creamy.

2. Transfer the mixture to a medium saucepan and cook over medium heat, stirring often, for 5 minutes. The mixture will become a sticky paste. Remove the saucepan from the heat and let cool for 10 minutes.

3. Lay out an 8-inch-long (20 cm) piece of plastic wrap. Transfer ½ cup (120 g) of the paste to the center of the plastic wrap. Bring the corners of the plastic wrap together and twist to close, making a little packet. Repeat with the remaining plantain mixture and more plastic wrap. Place the packets on a plate to cool for 20 minutes more.

4. Remove the plastic wrap and serve with jollof (if using).

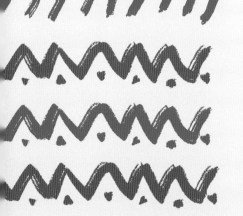

TWEENS ON THE SCENE (11+)

Peeling a plantain isn't as easy as peeling a banana. The outside is tougher, so grab your tween and a couple of safety knives and split the work, with everyone helping to wrestle the peels off the plantains.

CHIN CHIN

SERVES 4

¼ cup (50 g) granulated sugar

¼ cup (60 ml) evaporated milk

¼ cup (½ stick, or 55 g) salted butter, softened

2 cups (250 g) all-purpose flour, plus more for dusting

1 teaspoon salt

½ teaspoon baking powder

¼ teaspoon nutmeg

6 cups (1.4 kg) vegetable oil, for frying

1. In a small bowl, whisk together the sugar and evaporated milk until the sugar is dissolved.

2. In a large bowl, using a hand or stand mixer, cream the butter until light and fluffy on medium speed. Gradually add the flour, salt, baking powder, and nutmeg while continuing to stir. Add the milk mixture.

3. Switch to the dough hook and knead on low speed (or by hand) for 2 to 5 minutes, until the dough is smooth.

4. Lightly flour a clean work surface, then turn the dough out onto it. Using a floured rolling pin, roll the dough to ½-inch (12 mm) thickness. Use a pizza cutter or knife to slice ½-inch-thick (12 mm) lines in one direction, then ½-inch-thick (12 mm) lines in the opposite direction to create little squares.

5. Line a baking sheet with paper towels. Attach a deep-fry thermometer to the side of a large, heavy pot. Add the vegetable oil to the pot and heat over medium-high heat. Once the oil reaches 360°F (180°C), carefully add the dough squares, working in batches, and stir gently to keep them separate. Cook for 1 to 2 minutes, until golden brown. Use a slotted spoon to scoop the fried dough onto the prepared baking sheet. Let cool slightly and serve.

BIG KIDS IN THE KITCHEN (7+)

If you have a rolling pin with a thickness indicator, it makes rolling out dough easy for everyone, including your big kid. Just set the thickness to ½ inch (12 mm) and let them go to town!

SOMALIA WEEK

(INDEPENDENCE DAY, JULY 1)

Somalia, a small East African nation, has been significantly influenced by its Arab neighbors to the east, particularly in terms of culture and religion. Despite enduring political turmoil, the Somali people continue to thrive and create delicious dishes using locally sourced ingredients.

This week's recipes include bariis iskukaris, halva, and canjeero. BARIIS ISUKUKARIS is a lamb and rice dish that is perfect for serving to a large family. HALVA is a sweet and savory treat that tastes similar to hummus. CANJEERO is very similar to a French crêpe (page 158); these thin pancakes can hold your favorite fillings.

If you're unfamiliar with Somalia, now is a great time to learn more about their culture and practices. With a growing Somali immigrant population in the United States, you might be surprised to discover your neighbors may be from Somalia! Consider exploring Somali cuisine together and experiencing the rich flavors of their culinary heritage.

BARIIS ISKUKARIS

SERVES 6

- 1 tablespoon vegetable oil
- 1 pound (454 g) lamb meat, cubed
- 1 large yellow onion, sliced
- 1 tablespoon minced garlic
- 1 tablespoon minced fresh ginger
- 1 teaspoon ground cumin
- 1 teaspoon ground coriander
- 1 teaspoon ground turmeric
- ½ teaspoon salt
- ½ teaspoon ground black pepper
- 2 cups (330 g) cooked long-grain rice
- ½ cup (75 g) raisins
- ½ cup (120 ml) chicken broth

1. In a large skillet or wok, heat the oil over medium heat for 2 minutes. Place the lamb cubes in the pan and sear each side for about 2 minutes. Remove the meat from the pan.

2. Add the onion to the same pan and cook, stirring often, for about 5 minutes, or until soft. Add the garlic, ginger, cumin, coriander, turmeric, salt, and pepper. Stir until well combined.

3. Add the rice, raisins, broth, and seared lamb and stir. Bring the mixture to a boil over medium heat. Cover the pan, reduce the heat to low, and let simmer for 10 minutes.

4. Scoop into bowls and serve.

TWEENS ON THE SCENE (11+)

If you own a rice cooker, it might be time to show your tween how to use it. Rice cookers are very easy to use and create a consistent rice texture every time. Your tween can prepare the rice for this dish, and then any other rice dish in the future!

HALVA

SERVES 8

1½ cups (300 g) granulated
    sugar

½ teaspoon ground cardamom

1⅔ cups (400 ml) tahini

2 teaspoons vanilla extract

½ cup (60 g) chopped, roasted,
    and salted pistachios

1. Line a 5 by 9-inch (12 by 23 cm) dish with parchment paper.

2. In a medium pot, stir together the sugar, cardamom, and ¾ cup (180 ml) of water over medium heat. Bring to a boil, reduce the heat to low, and let simmer until the temperature reaches 250°F (120°C).

3. Remove the pot from the heat and stir in the tahini and vanilla until incorporated, then stir in the pistachios.

4. Pour the mixture into the prepared dish, using a spatula to smooth the top until the mixture is uniform. Cover and refrigerate for 4 hours.

5. Break into pieces or cut into squares and serve.

TWEENS ON THE SCENE (11+)

Reading a traditional thermometer can be tricky, but it is much easier to read a digital thermometer where the numbers are more clearly written out. Ask your tween to keep an eye on the thermometer and let you know when the temperature reaches 250°F (120°C).

CANJEERO

MAKES 8 CANJEERO

2 cups (250 g) self-rising flour

2 tablespoons powdered milk

1¼ teaspoons granulated sugar

1¼ teaspoons salt

1 teaspoon active dry yeast

1 large egg

½ cup (120 ml) vegetable oil, divided

Optional Fillings

Butter

Honey

Maple syrup

Sprinkles

Ham

Cheese

1. In a large bowl, using a hand or stand mixer on medium speed, beat the flour, milk powder, sugar, salt, yeast, egg, and 1⅓ cups (320 ml) of water until a thick batter forms, about 3 minutes.

2. Cover the batter with a clean kitchen towel and let sit at room temperature for 2 hours, or until it is bubbly.

3. In a large nonstick skillet, heat 1 tablespoon of the oil over medium heat. Scoop ½ cup (120 ml) of the batter into the center of the pan and use a ladle to swirl the batter outward like a crêpe. Cover the pan and cook for 1 to 2 minutes, until the underside is golden brown. Flip and cook for 30 seconds more, or until cooked through and golden.

4. Transfer to a serving platter, cover with a clean kitchen towel, and repeat step 3 with the remaining batter and oil. Top the canjeero with your favorite fillings.

BIG KIDS IN THE KITCHEN (7+)

Your big kid can decide on and serve the fillings, both sweet and savory, for the canjeero.

CANADA WEEK

As the United States' closest neighbor to the north, Canada offers a rich and diverse culture worth exploring. Here are some interesting facts about Canada:

- **SIZE.** Canada is the second-largest country in the world, surpassed only by Russia

- **COASTLINE.** Canada boasts the longest coastline of any nation.

- **LANGUAGES.** English and French are Canada's official languages.

- **NATIONAL ANIMAL.** The North American beaver is Canada's national animal. It was a prominent symbol of Canada even before the ever-present maple leaf.

- **SPORTS.** Canada has two official national sports: ice hockey for the winter and lacrosse for the summer.

- **MAPLE SYRUP.** Canada is the global leader in maple syrup production.

- **CANADA DAY.** Canadians celebrate their independence on July 1, a day known as Canada Day.

POUTINE

SERVES 6

1 bag (26 ounces, or 737 g) frozen french fries

3 cups (336 g) cheddar cheese curds

1 jar (18 ounces, or 510 g) beef gravy, warmed

Sliced green onions, for garnishing (optional)

1. Prepare the french fries according to package directions.

2. Divide the hot french fries among 6 bowls. Top each bowl with ½ cup (56 g) of the cheese curds. Drizzle each with hot gravy and sprinkle with green onions (if using). Serve immediately.

TWEENS ON THE SCENE (11+)

A great way to prepare frozen french fries is in an air fryer. Air fryers are basically tiny ovens that are able to get hotter much faster due to their compact size. Most frozen fry bags now have air fryer instructions on their labels, and your tween should be able to follow the instructions and cook up the fries!

BANNOCK

MAKES 4 BANNOCKS

2 cups (250 g) all-purpose flour, plus more for dusting

2 teaspoons baking powder

½ teaspoon salt

1 cup (240 ml) whole milk

½ cup (1 stick, or 115 g) butter, melted

Nonstick cooking spray

Optional Toppings
Butter

Jam

Honey

1. In the bowl of a stand mixer fitted with the paddle attachment on low speed, mix, add the flour, baking powder, and salt and stir. While continuing to mix on low speed, pour in the milk, followed by the butter.

2. Switch to the dough hook and knead on low speed for 4 minutes, or until the dough comes together in a ball.

3. Lightly flour a clean work surface, then turn the dough out onto it. Divide the dough into 4 equal balls. Use your hands or a rolling pin to flatten each ball to about ¼ inch (6 mm) thick; you can keep it round or make it oblong.

4. Coat a large skillet with nonstick cooking spray and cook the dough pieces, one at a time, over medium heat, 1 to 2 minutes per side, until golden. Serve warm with butter, jam, and/or honey.

BIG KIDS IN THE KITCHEN (7+)

Have your big kid help you flatten the dough balls. Instruct them to wet their hands with water and press the dough balls to be ¼ inch (6 mm) thick.

MAPLE SUGAR COOKIES

MAKES 12 COOKIES

Cookies

1 cup (2 sticks, or 230 g) salted butter, softened

¾ cup (180 ml) vegetable oil

2 cups (200 g) granulated sugar, plus more for coating

2 large eggs

2 tablespoons sour cream

1 teaspoon vanilla extract

½ teaspoon maple extract

½ teaspoon baking soda

1 teaspoon salt

5½ cups (690 g) all-purpose flour

Frosting

½ cup (1 stick, or 115 g) salted butter, softened

¼ cup (60 ml) sour cream

¼ cup (60 ml) pure maple syrup

2 pounds (910 g) confectioners' sugar

¼ cup (60 ml) heavy whipping cream

1. Preheat the oven to 350°F (180°C). Line a baking sheet with parchment paper.

2. To make the cookies: In a large bowl, using a hand or stand mixer, cream together the 1 cup (230 g) butter, oil, and granulated sugar on medium speed. Add the eggs, 2 tablespoons sour cream, and vanilla and maple extracts and mix until well combined. While continuing to mix, add the baking soda, salt, and flour and mix for 1 minute, or until well combined.

3. Use a large cookie scoop to scoop the dough into balls and place onto the prepared baking sheet. Take a flat-bottomed glass, dip the bottom into granulated sugar, and press it into a ball of dough to flatten to about ¼ inch (6 mm) thickness. Repeat with the remaining dough, dipping the glass in sugar each time after flattening.

4. Bake for 13 to 15 minutes, until the bottoms just begin to brown. Let cool completely on the baking sheet, about 45 minutes.

5. To make the frosting: In the bowl of a stand mixer fitted with the whisk attachment, cream the ½ cup (115 g) butter, ¼ cup (60 ml) sour cream, and maple syrup for 2 minutes, then gradually add the confectioners' sugar while continuing to mix. Keep mixing and drizzle in the whipping cream until a thick frosting forms.

6. Once the cookies are cooled, cover each one with a generous amount of frosting and serve immediately.

LITTLE HELPING HANDS (3+)

Your little helper can do the job of smushing each of the cookies down with the sugared cup.

AMERICAN FARE WEEK

(INDEPENDENCE DAY, JULY 4)

"The land of the free and the home of the brave"—these words from "The Star-Spangled Banner," penned by Francis Scott Key, honor the American flag and its iconic stars and stripes. It's American Fare Week! A time when hot dogs are sizzling and the colors red, white, and blue are everywhere.

Many foods we consider quintessentially American have roots in other parts of the world, such as hamburgers and hot dogs. This is not surprising, considering America's relatively young history as a nation finding its place on the global stage.

It's important to remember that America has a history dating back centuries, long before the arrival of Columbus. The land was already inhabited and cherished by numerous Native American tribes. When we speak of America, the story doesn't begin with discovery, as the land was already being lived on and loved.

As you celebrate the Fourth of July, take a moment to reflect on the experiences of Native Americans, the colonists' struggle for freedom from England, and the ongoing sacrifices of troops ensuring our enduring freedom.

SPIRAL HOT DOGS AND SAUCE

SERVES 6

¾ cup (165 g) brown sugar

¾ cup (180 ml) ketchup

½ cup (120 ml) honey

½ teaspoon onion powder

1 teaspoon Worcestershire sauce

1 teaspoon apple cider vinegar

6 beef hot dogs

6 hot dog buns

1. In a small saucepan, bring the brown sugar, ketchup, honey, onion powder, Worcestershire sauce, and apple cider vinegar to a boil over medium heat. Remove the sauce from the heat and let cool completely, about 1 hour.

2. Working with one hot dog at a time, start at one tip and drag a knife just through the skin of the hot dog while twisting it, to spiral down to the opposite tip. Repeat with all the remaining hot dogs. Poke each hot dog 3 or 4 times with a fork.

3. Place the hot dogs on a microwave-safe plate and microwave for 30 seconds to 1 minute, until warmed through (see Note). Serve with the ketchup–brown sugar sauce.

NOTE

THIS COOKING METHOD IS QUICK AND EASY, BUT IF YOU PREFER YOUR HOT DOGS BOILED, STEAMED, GRILLED, OR COOKED IN A HOT DOG COOKER, THOSE WAYS ARE GREAT TOO!

BIG KIDS IN THE KITCHEN (7+)

A hot dog cooker is a fun kitchen appliance that only cooks one thing, but it gives kids the ability and confidence to cook hot dogs on their own, which is a kid-favorite food for sure. Usually, the cooker just requires adding some water to a reservoir and then placing in the hot dogs to steam. Just be sure to help them remove the cooked hot dogs to avoid steam burns!

FOURTH OF JULY PARFAITS

MAKES 6 PARFAITS

2 cups (480 ml) boiling water, divided

1 box (3 ounces, or 85 g) blue raspberry–flavored gelatin

2 cups (480 ml) cold water, divided

1 box (3 ounces, or 85 g) cherry-flavored gelatin

1 tub (8 ounces, or 227 g) frozen whipped topping, thawed

12 strawberries, hulled and quartered

1 cup (145 g) blueberries

1. In a large bowl, whisk together 1 cup (240 ml) of the boiling water and the blue raspberry gelatin. Whisk for about 2 minutes, or until everything dissolves. Add 1 cup (240 ml) of the cold water and whisk again for 30 seconds. Divide the mixture equally into 6 clear, tall, heatproof glasses and refrigerate to set, at least 4 hours and up to overnight.

2. In a clean large bowl, combine the remaining 1 cup (240 ml) boiling water and the cherry gelatin. Whisk for about 2 minutes, or until everything dissolves. Add the remaining 1 cup (240 ml) cold water and whisk again for 30 seconds.

3. Pour the mixture gently into an 8 by 8-inch (20 by 20 cm) glass dish and refrigerate to set, at least 4 hours and up to overnight.

4. Use a knife to cut the cherry gelatin into ½-inch (12 mm) cubes.

5. Scoop about 2 tablespoons of the whipped topping on top of the blue raspberry gelatin in each cup and smooth down. Arrange 4 cubes of the cherry gelatin on the whipped topping against the sides of the cup (eat or discard any excess cherry gelatin), then scoop more whipped topping into each cup until the topping is flush with the top of the cup.

6. Place the sliced strawberries and blueberries onto the top of each cup and serve immediately.

BIG KIDS IN THE KITCHEN (7+)

Hulling and prepping the strawberries is a great job for a big kid using a safety knife.

TRIPLE LAYER SLUSHES

MAKES 4 SLUSHES

6 cups (940 g) crushed ice, divided

8 ounces (240 ml) blue raspberry syrup

4 ounces (120 ml) lemon syrup

4 ounces (120 ml) lime syrup

1 ounce (30 ml) grenadine syrup

¼ cup (28 g) cherry-flavored popping boba balls

1. In a blender, combine 3 cups (420 g) of the crushed ice and the blue raspberry syrup and process on high until smooth, 1 to 2 minutes. Divide among 4 clear plastic cups. Rinse the blender.

2. In the clean blender, combine the remaining 3 cups (420 g) crushed ice and the lemon and lime syrups and process until smooth, 1 to 2 minutes. Pour on top of the blue slush in the cups.

3. Drizzle the slushes with the grenadine and sprinkle with the popping boba balls. Serve immediately with a wide straw.

BUDDING SOUS-CHEFS (17+)

Specific flavored syrups and boba balls can be tough to find in retail stores but are easily accessible online. Have your young adult help you pick out these items online and then make the slush together.

FRANCE WEEK

(BASTILLE DAY, JULY 14)

France is renowned for its exquisite cuisine, particularly its sophisticated and innovative dishes. As the world's top tourist destination, France welcomes visitors with a plethora of delectable culinary offerings.

July 14 marks Bastille Day in France, commemorating the Storming of the Bastille in 1789. This pivotal event, where revolutionaries stormed the fortress-prison, ignited the French Revolution and led to the end of the monarchy. Today, Bastille Day is celebrated with parades, fireworks, picnics, and festivities across the country. Here are a few simple French phrases you can incorporate into your week:

MERCI
(mehr-see): Thank-you

"BONJOUR"
(bown-zhoor): Hello

S'IL VOUS PLAIT
(sil-voo-play): Please

AU REVOIR
(oh-ruhv-waa): Goodbye

Remember to use *s'il vous plaît* when requesting a baguette sandwich and express your gratitude with a *merci* after enjoying your crêpes!

CRÊPES

MAKES 4 CRÊPES

1 cup (125 g) all-purpose flour

2 large eggs

¾ cup (180 ml) whole milk

½ teaspoon salt

2 tablespoons salted butter, melted

Nonstick cooking spray

Optional Fillings

Chocolate hazelnut spread (such as Nutella)

Jam

Nuts

Sliced bananas

Sliced strawberries

Chopped cooked ham and Swiss cheese

Chopped cooked chicken and barbecue sauce

1. In a food processor or blender, process the flour, eggs, milk, salt, and butter for about 1 minute, or until well combined.

2. Preheat an electric crêpe pan or a large skillet and grease with nonstick cooking spray. Pouring directly from the blender, swirl ¼ to ½ cup (60 to 120 ml) of the batter to coat the bottom of the pan. Pick up the pan by the handle and tilt the pan to get the batter all the way to the edges.

3. Cook for about 2 minutes, then slide a spatula around the outside edges and flip the crêpe to cook on the opposite side for 2 minutes more. Transfer the crêpe to a large plate and repeat with the remaining batter, spraying the pan after each crêpe.

4. To eat, place one crêpe on a plate and add any fillings you like. Fold into quarters or roll and enjoy with a fork.

TWEENS ON THE SCENE (11+)

Let your tween get creative and choose the toppings, both sweet and savory options, for the crêpes.

BAGUETTE SANDWICH

MAKES 4 SANDWICHES

½ cup (1 stick, or 115 g) salted butter, softened

1 teaspoon flaky salt

2 teaspoons garlic powder

2 teaspoons herbes de Provence

1 long baguette

4 slices prosciutto

4 slices honey ham

1 wheel (8 ounces, or 227 g) Brie cheese, sliced

2 cups (40 g) arugula

1. Place an oven rack 3 inches (7.5 cm) from the heat source and preheat the broiler.

2. In a small bowl, mix the butter with the flaky salt, garlic powder, and herbes de Provence until well combined.

3. Slice open the baguette lengthwise and spread the insides with the butter mixture. Lay the slices of prosciutto and ham on the bottom half, then lay the Brie slices on top of the meat.

4. Transfer the sandwich to a baking sheet and broil, open-faced, for 2 to 4 minutes, until the Brie is melty.

5. Remove from the oven, arrange the arugula on top of the Brie, and press the bread together to close the sandwich. Slice into 4 equal pieces and serve.

TWEENS ON THE SCENE (11+)

Adding ingredients to butter turns it into compound butter. Have your tween make the compound butter. Though salt, garlic powder, and herbes de Provence make a lovely compound butter, but encourage your tween to experiment with other herbs and spices to create a masterpiece of their own design.

STEAK FRITES

SERVES 4

4 steaks (6 ounces, or 170 g, each)

1 tablespoon flaky salt

1 teaspoon ground black pepper

½ cup (1 stick, or 115 g) salted butter, softened

4 cups (228 g) frozen french fries

¼ cup (60 ml) garlic aioli

1. Preheat an air fryer to 400°F (200°C).

2. Season the steaks all over with the salt and pepper. Smear both sides of each steak with the butter, then add the steaks to the basket of the air fryer and cook for 10 minutes. Flip and cook 10 minutes more, or until the internal temperature reaches your desired doneness, 135°F (55°C) for medium.

3. Remove from the air fryer and rest the steaks on a cutting board for 10 minutes.

4. Meanwhile, cook the french fries in the air fryer following package directions.

5. Slice the steak against the grain into ¼-inch (6 mm) slices.

6. Serve with the french fries and drizzle everything with the garlic aioli.

BIG KIDS IN THE KITCHEN (7+)

Let your big kids prep the steaks with the salt, pepper, and butter. Using a butter knife or a wooden spreader makes the job easy and safe.

"FOWL" PLAY WEEK

Chicken is a protein that's both versatile and nutritious. It's a great option for families, especially those with picky eaters, as it can be prepared in countless ways. This week, we're celebrating all things chicken!

The recipes in this section are kid-friendly and delicious. Try them out and let your little ones vote on their favorites to add to your regular meal rotation. Cluck-a-doodle-doo! Here are some jokes to share:

- **WHAT DO YOU CALL A PRANKSTER CHICKEN?**
  A practical yolker!

- **WHAT IS A CHICKEN'S FAVORITE VEGETABLE?**
  Eggplant!

- **WHAT IS A CHICKEN'S FAVORITE DESSERT?**
  Coop-Cakes!

AIR FRYER WINGS

MAKES 20 WINGS

½ cup (120 ml) honey

2 tablespoons favorite barbecue sauce

4 teaspoons minced garlic

1 teaspoon minced fresh ginger

20 frozen breaded chicken wings

1. Preheat an air fryer to 400°F (200°C).

2. In a large bowl, stir together the honey, barbecue sauce, garlic, and ginger.

3. Add the frozen wings to the air fryer basket and cook for 10 minutes, then flip and cook for an additional 6 to 10 minutes, until the internal temperature reaches 165°F (75°C).

4. Pour the cooked wings into the sauce and toss to coat. Serve immediately.

BIG KIDS IN THE KITCHEN (7+)

Your big kid can stir the sauce ingredients together and toss the wings in the sauce once they are cooked. Just explain that the wings are hot and not to touch them too soon!

CHICKEN PILLOWS

MAKES 8 PILLOWS

Chicken Pillows

3 cups (585 g) shredded cooked chicken

1 package (8 ounces, or 227 g) cream cheese, softened

2 tablespoons salted butter, softened

1 can (8 ounces, or 227 g) refrigerated crescent roll dough

6 cups (168 g) corn flakes

⅓ cup (75 g) salted butter, melted

Topping

1 can (10.5 ounces, or 298 g) cream of chicken soup

½ cup (120 ml) sour cream

TWEENS ON THE SCENE (11+)

Have your tween wrap up the filling into the crescent rolls. Just explain that they have to seal all the edges really well, or the filling will bubble and leak out!

1. Preheat the oven to 350°F (180°C). Line a large baking sheet with parchment paper.

2. **To make the chicken pillows:** In a large bowl, stir together the chicken, cream cheese, and softened butter.

3. Roll out the crescent dough on a clean work surface. Working with one dough triangle at a time, scoop about ⅓ cup (80 g) chicken filling onto the center of the triangle and wrap the corners and edges around the filling, pinching everywhere to seal. Repeat with the remaining triangles and filling and place on the prepared baking sheet.

4. Place the corn flakes in a large zip-top plastic bag and seal, then use a rolling pin or the backside of a skillet to gently crush the corn flakes into large crumbs.

5. Working with one pillow at a time, dip the pillow in the melted butter, then roll it in the crushed corn flakes to coat all around the outside of the dough. Place back onto the baking sheet and repeat with the remaining pillows.

6. Bake for 20 to 25 minutes, until the outside is golden brown.

7. **While baking, prepare the topping:** In a small saucepan, combine the cream of chicken soup and sour cream over medium heat and cook, stirring, for 2 to 3 minutes, until just warm. Remove the pan from the heat.

8. Drizzle the topping over the chicken pillows and serve immediately.

CHICKIE NUGGIES

MAKES 40 NUGGIES

1 cup (100 g) Italian-style bread crumbs

½ cup (50 g) grated Parmesan cheese

1 tablespoon dried basil

1 teaspoon dried thyme

1 teaspoon salt

3 boneless, skinless chicken breasts, cut into 1-inch (2.5 cm) cubes

½ cup (1 stick, or 115 g) butter, melted

Favorite dipping sauce(s), for serving

1. Preheat the oven to 400°F (200°C). Line a baking sheet with parchment paper.

2. In a medium bowl, stir together the bread crumbs, Parmesan, basil, thyme, and salt.

3. Dip the chicken pieces, one at a time, in the butter, then the bread crumbs, and then place on the prepared baking sheet. Discard any excess bread crumbs.

4. Bake for 20 to 25 minutes, until the internal temperature reaches 165°F (75°C). Serve with your favorite dipping sauce(s).

LITTLE HELPING HANDS (3+)

Your little helper can do the chicken breading, but to make it even more sanitary (and fun) consider buying kid-size disposable gloves. When working with possible bacteria-carrying foods like raw chicken, gloves can help protect your littles.

SWEDEN WEEK

(MIDSOMMAR)

On a Friday between June 19 and 25 each year, Sweden celebrates Midsommar, a joyous festival marking the summer solstice. Rooted in ancient pagan traditions, this holiday is filled with dancing around a maypole, feasting on traditional foods, lighting bonfires, and adorning oneself with flower crowns. If you're eager to create your own flower crown for Sweden Week, here's a simple guide:

1. CREATE THE BASE. Form a circular wire frame that fits loosely around your head. Wrap the entire wire in green floral tape.

2. ADD GREENERY. Select greenery from your garden or purchase it from a florist. Secure it to the wire frame using floral tape.

3. INCORPORATE FLOWERS. Choose your favorite blooms and attach them to the greenery using floral tape.

4. WEAR WITH PRIDE. Once complete, proudly wear your handmade flower crown.

If you prefer a more durable crown, consider using artificial flowers. These can be purchased at craft stores and reused year after year.

MEATBALLS

MAKES 20 TO 30 MEATBALLS

Meatballs

Nonstick cooking spray

1 pound (454 g) ground beef

½ pound (227 g) ground pork

½ cup (50 g) plain dried bread crumbs

½ cup (65 g) finely chopped yellow onion

½ cup (120 ml) whole milk

1 teaspoon salt

1 teaspoon granulated sugar

½ teaspoon ground black pepper

¼ teaspoon ground ginger

¼ teaspoon ground nutmeg

¼ teaspoon ground allspice

1 large egg

Gravy

1 tablespoon butter

1 tablespoon all-purpose flour

½ cup (120 ml) beef stock

½ cup (120 ml) heavy cream

½ teaspoon Dijon mustard

½ teaspoon Worcestershire sauce

¼ teaspoon ground black pepper

For Serving & Garnishing

Mashed Potatoes (page 248) (optional)

Fresh parsley leaves (optional)

1. Preheat the oven to 400°F (200°C). Place a wire cooling rack on top of a baking sheet and spray it with nonstick cooking spray.

2. To make the meatballs: In a large bowl, mix the beef, pork, bread crumbs, onion, milk, salt, sugar, ½ teaspoon pepper, ginger, nutmeg, allspice, and egg until well combined. Use a spoon or cookie scoop to scoop approximately 2 tablespoons of meat mixture. Roll it into a ball and place on the prepared cooling rack. Repeat with the remaining meat mixture, leaving a little space between the balls on the rack.

3. Bake for 15 to 20 minutes, until the internal temperature of the meat at the thickest point reaches 160°F (70°C).

4. Meanwhile, make the gravy: In a small saucepan, melt the butter over medium heat. Once bubbling, add the flour and cook, stirring constantly, for 30 seconds.

5. Slowly whisk in the beef stock, cream, Dijon, Worcestershire sauce, and ¼ teaspoon black pepper. Reduce the heat to medium-low and let cook for about 5 minutes, until thickened (enough to coat the back of a spoon), stirring often.

6. Place a large scoop of mashed potatoes (if using) on each plate, then top with 2 or 3 meatballs, drizzle with the gravy, and garnish with parsley (if using).

TWEENS ON THE SCENE (11+)

Your tween will be a great helper to get their hands right into the meat! Have them squish all around until all the spices and seasonings are mixed up, then show them how to form the meat into balls. This can be done with or without gloves, depending on your tween's preference.

PICKLED VEGETABLES

SERVES 6

½ pound (227 g) cucumbers, sliced into spears

½ pound (227 g) carrots, peeled and sliced into sticks

1 cup (240 ml) white vinegar

⅓ cup (65 g) granulated sugar

1 tablespoon salt

½ teaspoon ground mustard

1 teaspoon chopped fresh dill

1 bay leaf

1. Arrange the cucumbers and carrots in a quart-size (960 ml) mason jar with a lid.

2. In a small saucepan, bring 1 cup (240 ml) of water and the white vinegar, sugar, salt, mustard, dill, and bay leaf to a boil over medium heat. Reduce the heat to low and let simmer for 5 minutes. Remove from the heat.

3. Carefully pour the hot mixture over the vegetables in the jar. The vegetables should be completely covered in hot liquid.

4. Place the lid on the jar lightly and let the mixture cool to room temperature, about 2 hours.

5. Transfer to the refrigerator for even deeper flavor penetration. Pickles will keep in the refrigerator for up to 1 month unopened and up to 2 weeks after opening.

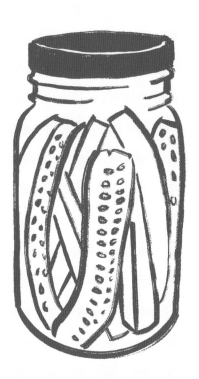

LITTLE HELPING HANDS (3+)

Your little helper can shove the vegetables into the jar, just explain that they will all fit better if they stand up straight next to one another. You can buy pre-cut carrot sticks at the grocery store to make prep even easier.

STRAWBERRY CAKE

SERVES 8

Sponge Cake

Nonstick cooking spray

6 large eggs

1¼ cups (250 g) granulated sugar

1¼ cups (155 g) all-purpose flour

1 teaspoon vanilla extract

¼ teaspoon almond extract

Strawberry Filling

2 cups (330 g) fresh strawberries, hulled and chopped

½ cup (100 g) granulated sugar

1 tablespoon fresh lemon juice

1 tablespoon cornstarch

Topping

1 pint (480 ml) heavy whipping cream

¼ cup (30 g) confectioners' sugar

1 teaspoon vanilla extract

8 large strawberries, stems on

1. Preheat the oven to 350°F (180°C). Grease two 8 by 8-inch (20 by 20 cm) cake pans with nonstick cooking spray and line the bottoms and sides of each pan with parchment paper.

2. To make the cake: In a large bowl, using a hand or stand mixer on medium speed, beat the eggs and 1¼ cups (250 g) granulated sugar until creamy. Add the flour and vanilla and almond extracts and mix for 1 minute more. Divide the batter between the two prepared cake pans.

3. Bake 25 to 35 minutes, until a toothpick inserted in the center comes out clean. Let the cakes cool completely in their pans, about 1 hour.

4. Meanwhile, make the strawberry filling: In a small saucepan, bring the chopped strawberries, ½ cup (50 g) granulated sugar, lemon juice, cornstarch, and ¼ cup (60 ml) of water to a boil over medium heat. Reduce the heat to low and let simmer for 10 minutes to thicken. Remove the pan from the heat and pour the filling into a heatproof bowl. Lightly cover, then refrigerate for 1 hour.

5. To make the topping: In a clean bowl of the stand mixer fitted with the whisk attachment, add the cream, confectioners' sugar, and vanilla and whip on high speed for about 3 minutes, or until stiff peaks form.

6. To assemble the cake, place one of the cooled cake rounds on a plate and scoop half of the strawberry filling onto it and smooth it over the cake. Place the second cake round on top of the filling and spread the whipped topping all over it like frosting. Drizzle the top with the remaining strawberry filling and decorate with the whole strawberries. Slice and serve immediately.

TWEENS ON THE SCENE (11+)

Allow your tween to make the topping and decide when the peaks are stiff enough.

JAMAICA WEEK

(INDEPENDENCE DAY, AUGUST 6)

August 6 marks Jamaica's Independence Day, a celebration of the nation's liberation from British rule in 1962. For over 300 years, the island nation was under British colonial control.

Jamaica is renowned for its vibrant culture, delicious cuisine, and iconic music. One of the most famous Jamaicans is Bob Marley, a legendary singer-songwriter whose music has left an enduring impact on the world. Listen to some of his popular songs, such as "Jamming," "Buffalo Soldier," "Three Little Birds," and "Stir It Up," to immerse yourself in the Jamaican vibe.

As you cook the week's delectable island dishes with your family, let the rhythm of Jamaican music fill your kitchen and inspire your culinary creations.

JERK CHICKEN

SERVES 6

½ cup (48 g) jerk seasoning

¼ cup (60 ml) olive oil

1 tablespoon brown sugar

1 tablespoon fresh lime juice

1 teaspoon garlic powder

1 teaspoon onion powder

½ teaspoon ground allspice

¼ teaspoon cayenne pepper

6 bone-in, skin-on chicken thighs

Cucumber Mango Basil Slaw
(page 183), for serving
(optional)

1. In a large bowl, whisk together the jerk seasoning, oil, brown sugar, lime juice, garlic powder, onion powder, allspice, and cayenne until a thick paste forms.

2. Add the chicken to the bowl and toss to coat. Cover and marinate in the refrigerator for at least 1 hour or up to overnight.

3. Preheat a grill to medium heat or place a grill pan over medium heat. Place the chicken pieces on the grill, skin sides down, and cook for 8 to 10 minutes, then flip and cook for 5 to 8 minutes more, until the internal temperature reaches 165°F (75°C). Remove from the grill and serve with cucumber mango basil slaw (if using).

LITTLE HELPING HANDS (3+)

Let your little helper hold onto the big bowl and whisk after you put each ingredient into the bowl. Be sure to explain what each ingredient is and let them smell each one so they understand what is in the marinade.

SORREL

SERVES 4

1 cup (30 g) dried hibiscus
  flowers (see Note)

1½ cups (300 g) granulated
  sugar

1 cinnamon stick

½ teaspoon ground cloves

¼ teaspoon ground nutmeg

2 tablespoons fresh lime juice

Fresh lime wedges or wheels,
  for serving

1. In a medium pot, add the flowers and 6 cups (1.4 L) of water over medium heat. Bring to a boil, then reduce the heat to low and let simmer for 10 minutes.

2. Remove from the heat and add the sugar, cinnamon stick, cloves, and nutmeg. Let the mixture cool completely in the pot, about 30 minutes,

3. Strain the mixture through a fine-mesh sieve into a pitcher. Stir in the lime juice. Serve by pouring over ice into glasses. Garnish with lime wedges or wheels.

NOTE

DRIED HIBISCUS FLOWERS MAY BE HARD TO FIND IN US GROCERY STORES, SO CHECK ONLINE WHERE THERE SHOULD BE PLENTY OF OPTIONS.

BIG KIDS IN THE KITCHEN (7+)

Have your big kid get out glasses for everyone and fill them with ice cubes. You can even have them slice the limes with a safety knife and garnish the glasses if they would like!

COCONUT DROPS

MAKES 10 DROPS

2 cups (440 g) brown sugar

1 teaspoon ground cinnamon

½ teaspoon vanilla extract

2 teaspoons minced fresh ginger

1 bag (7 ounces, or 198 g)
   flaked coconut

1. Line a cookie sheet with parchment paper.

2. In a medium saucepan, stir together the brown sugar, cinnamon, vanilla, ginger, and 2½ cups (600 ml) of water over medium heat until well combined. Stir in the coconut and bring to a boil. Reduce the heat to low and let simmer for about 10 minutes, or until the temperature reaches 280°F (140°C).

3. Carefully scoop the batter into 10 even lumps on the prepared cookie sheet. Let the drops cool completely on the pan, about 30 minutes, then serve. Store in an airtight container at room temperature for up to 4 days.

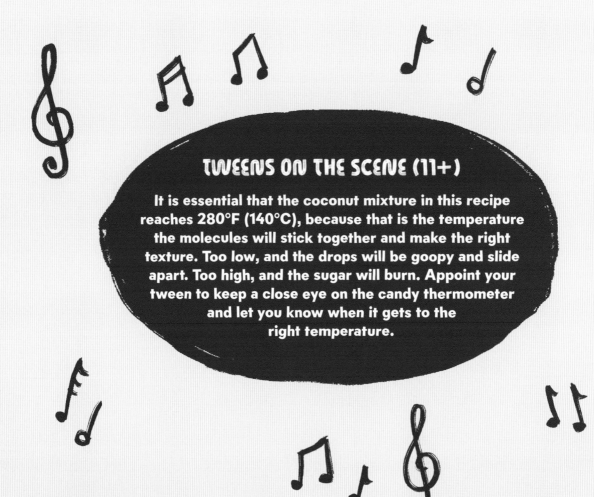

TWEENS ON THE SCENE (11+)

It is essential that the coconut mixture in this recipe reaches 280°F (140°C), because that is the temperature the molecules will stick together and make the right texture. Too low, and the drops will be goopy and slide apart. Too high, and the sugar will burn. Appoint your tween to keep a close eye on the candy thermometer and let you know when it gets to the right temperature.

ARGENTINA WEEK

Argentina's diverse geography, ranging from vast plains to towering mountains, has shaped its cuisine and culture. From the mouthwatering steaks of the Pampas to the delectable seafood of Patagonia, Argentina offers a culinary journey like no other.

Apart from its geographic features, Argentina has also gained its influences from its diverse mix of people. Spanish conquistadors colonized Argentina in the sixteenth century, but the heart of the Indigenous people (including the Mapuche, Tehuelche, and Inca) live on in their customs, designs, and cuisine.

One of Argentina's most iconic cultural exports is the tango, a passionate and sensual dance characterized by its dramatic movements and close embrace. Watching professional tango dancers can inspire you to try your hand at this elegant dance form.

EMPANADAS

MAKES 12 EMPANADAS

½ pound (227 g) ground beef

½ medium white onion, diced

1 teaspoon minced garlic

1 green bell pepper, seeded and diced

¼ teaspoon ground cumin

¼ teaspoon chili powder

½ teaspoon salt

¼ teaspoon ground black pepper

2 packages (2 crusts per pack; 15 ounces, or 425 g, each) refrigerated piecrust dough, thawed

All-purpose flour, for dusting

1 large egg

Chimichurri or salsa verde, for serving

1. Preheat the oven to 400°F (200°C). Line a baking sheet with parchment paper.

2. In a large skillet, brown the ground beef over medium heat, while breaking it up with a wooden spoon, for 5 to 8 minutes, until cooked through.

3. Add the onion, garlic, and bell pepper and cook for about 5 minutes, or until softened. Stir in the cumin, chili powder, salt, and black pepper, then remove the pan from the heat. Let cool slightly, about 20 minutes.

4. Lightly flour a clean work surface. Using a floured rolling pin, roll out the 4 piecrusts. Use a 3-inch (7.5 cm) round biscuit or cookie cutter to cut out 12 circles. Discard excess dough.

5. Working with one dough circle at a time, place 1 to 2 tablespoons of the beef filling in the middle. Run a wet finger around the circumference of the circle and fold the dough in half to cover the filling. Use a fork to crimp the edges to keep the filling inside. Repeat with the remaining dough circles and filling.

6. Lay the empanadas on the prepared baking sheet. Beat the egg with 1 tablespoon of water in a small bowl, then brush the egg wash over the top of the empanadas.

7. Bake for 20 to 25 minutes, until the tops are golden brown. Serve immediately with chimichurri or salsa verde for dipping.

BIG KIDS IN THE KITCHEN (7+)

Hand your big kid a fork and put them on crimping duty! Show them how pressing the fork into the dough locks the layers of dough into each other.

MINT LEMONADE

SERVES 4

1 cup (200 g) granulated sugar

¾ cup (180 ml) fresh lemon juice (about 4 lemons)

10 fresh mint leaves

Ice

1. In a medium saucepan, stir together the sugar and 4 cups (960 ml) of water over medium heat. Cook until all the sugar is dissolved, then remove the pan from the heat. Let completely cool in the refrigerator, about 2 hours.

2. Pour the cooled sugar mixture into a pitcher, add the lemon juice and mint leaves, and stir. Let sit in the refrigerator for at least 1 hour and up to overnight to infuse. Pour into glasses of ice and serve.

TIP

FOR A FUN VARIATION, TRY MUDDLING SOME FRUIT AND ADDING IT TO THE LEMONADE. HULLED STRAWBERRIES OR RASPBERRIES (ABOUT ¼ CUP, OR 35 G) ADD A YUMMY AND SWEET TWIST.

TWEENS ON THE SCENE (11+)

If you have a hand-press style lemon juicer, your tween is going to have to bring their muscles to get all the juice out of those lemons!

DULCE DE LECHE

SERVES 6

1 can (14 ounces, or 400 g) sweetened condensed milk, unopened

Brownie Bites (page 103), Fizzy Berry Delight (page 16), Sweet Vareniki (page 21), or ice cream, for serving

1. Place the unopened can of sweetened condensed milk in a slow cooker and add water to the pot until it covers the can completely (about 5 cups, or 1.1 L). Place the lid on the slow cooker and cook on low for 9 hours.

2. Carefully remove the unopened can with tongs and place it on a hot pad to cool completely, about 1 hour. Open the can carefully and serve it as a dip or a topping for the brownie bites, fizzy berry delight, sweet vareniki, or ice cream.

BIG KIDS IN THE KITCHEN (7+)

This recipe is more like a magic trick. The can goes into the slow cooker as sweetened condensed milk and comes out as dulce de leche! Your big kid can make this recipe themselves; just help them remove the hot can and open it for them once it has cooled.

BARBECUE WEEK

Whether done with a grill or smoker, barbecuing is a special cooking method that infuses food with the smoky flavor of fire and wood. Even without an outdoor grill or smoker, you can recreate these recipes using a stovetop grill pan or skillet.

Barbecued is a global pastime, enjoyed in various cultures. In Australia, seafood like prawns and fish are grilled on the "barbie," while in Brazil, churrascaria restaurants feature skewered meats cooked over open flames. In Germany, grilled sausages are a popular choice. No matter where you are, barbecue is best enjoyed with friends and family. To enhance your barbecue experience, consider incorporating some fun lawn games:

- **CORNHOLE.** This is a classic game of skill and luck that involves tossing bean bags into a hole on a raised platform.

- **JENGA.** For a more physically demanding challenge, try building an oversized Jenga tower using two by fours.

- **FRISBEE OR KICKBALL.** And for a simple activity, a good old-fashioned game of Frisbee or kickball can't be beat.

CUCUMBER MANGO BASIL SLAW

SERVES 6

1 cup (70 g) thinly sliced napa cabbage

1 cup (95 g) thinly sliced red cabbage

½ medium ripe mango, peeled, pitted, and thinly sliced

½ medium cucumber, peeled and thinly sliced

3 fresh basil leaves, thinly sliced

½ cup (55 g) shredded carrots

¼ cup (10 g) minced fresh cilantro

1 tablespoon rice vinegar

1 tablespoon fresh lime juice

1 tablespoon vegetable oil

1 tablespoon sweet chili sauce

2 teaspoons granulated sugar

½ teaspoon sesame oil

Barbecued Chicken (page 184), hamburgers, or hot dogs, for serving

1. In a large bowl, mix the napa cabbage, red cabbage, mango, cucumber, basil, carrots, and cilantro.

2. In a small bowl, stir together the vinegar, lime juice, vegetable oil, chili sauce, sugar, and sesame oil.

3. Drizzle the sauce over the cabbage mixture and toss to combine.

4. Serve as a side with barbecued chicken or pile onto a burger or hot dog.

TWEENS ON THE SCENE (11+)

Mangos can be very tricky to work with as they are slimy, and the pit is firmly attached to the meat inside. To make things easier, try looking for pre-cut mangoes in the produce section of the grocery store. Then your tween can easily prep the other ingredients in this recipe with a safety knife and add the ready-prepped mangoes.

BARBECUED CHICKEN

SERVES 4

½ cup (120 ml) favorite barbecue sauce

¼ cup (55 g) brown sugar

¼ cup (60 ml) apple cider vinegar

1 tablespoon Worcestershire sauce

1 teaspoon smoked paprika

½ teaspoon garlic powder

¼ teaspoon onion powder

4 bone-in, skin-on chicken thighs

Cucumber Mango Basil Slaw (page 183; pictured opposite), for serving (optional)

1. In a large bowl, stir together the barbecue sauce, brown sugar, vinegar, Worcestershire sauce, paprika, garlic powder, and onion powder. Add the chicken to the bowl and toss to coat. Cover and marinate in the refrigerator for at least 30 minutes and up to overnight.

2. Preheat a grill to medium heat.

3. Grill for 25 to 30 minutes, flipping halfway through, until the internal temperature reaches 165°F (75°C).

4. Serve immediately with cucumber mango basil slaw (if using).

LITTLE HELPING HANDS (3+)

There are lots of choices for barbecue sauce at the grocery store. Take your little helper along with you to pick out the flavor they want, making sure to point out the different features of each for them to consider.

ST. LOUIS-STYLE RIBS

SERVES 4

1 rack (3 pounds, or 1.4 kg) pork back ribs

½ cup (120 ml) favorite barbecue sauce

¼ cup (55 g) brown sugar

¼ cup (60 ml) apple cider vinegar

1 tablespoon Worcestershire sauce

1 teaspoon paprika

½ teaspoon garlic powder

½ teaspoon onion powder

Cucumber Mango Basil Slaw (page 183), for serving (optional)

NOTE

IF YOU DON'T OWN A SMOKER, USE A GRILL INSTEAD. PREHEAT ONE SIDE OF YOUR GRILL TO 300°F (150°C) AND PLACE THE RIBS, BONE SIDE DOWN, ON THE UNHEATED SIDE. COOK FOR 1½ HOURS, THEN FLIP AND COOK AN ADDITIONAL 1½ HOURS. BRUSH WITH THE REMAINING SAUCE AND MOVE TO THE HEATED SIDE FOR 2 TO 5 MINUTES, UNTIL THE SAUCE IS BUBBLY.

1. Preheat a smoker to 225°F (110°C) (see Note).

2. Place the ribs on a large baking sheet and peel the membrane off the back side of the rack.

3. In a small bowl, stir together the barbecue sauce, brown sugar, vinegar, Worcestershire sauce, paprika, garlic powder, and onion powder. Pour the mixture all over the ribs, reserving about ¼ cup (60 ml) for later. Brush the mixture over the ribs and wash the brush thoroughly after using.

4. Place the ribs, meat side up, directly onto the rack in the smoker and smoke for about 3 hours. Use a meat thermometer to make sure the cooked ribs are at least 190°F (90°C).

5. Carefully remove the ribs and cover them in foil. Return them to the smoker for another 1 hour, or until the meat easily comes off the bones.

6. Using the clean brush, spread on the reserved sauce and serve with cucumber mango basil slaw (if using).

BIG KIDS IN THE KITCHEN (7+)

Give your big kids the ingredients to make the sauce and have them stir them together. They can also brush it all over the ribs. They will love painting the ribs with the sauce!

SPAIN WEEK

(LA TOMATINA)

¡Hola! It's Spain Week! So, grab your matador hat and get ready to savor some delicious Spanish cuisine.

Every August, the vibrant town of Buñol, Spain, hosts La Tomatina, the world's largest food fight. Thousands of people gather to hurl tomatoes at each other in a chaotic and fun-filled frenzy. As trucks filled with ripe tomatoes roll into the city center, the crowd transforms into a sea of red, embracing the playful spirit of this unique tradition.

Spain has a rich culinary landscape with foods highlighting their local agriculture and traditions. Food is the heart of Spain, and you will feel that in your home this week when you make tortilla española, paella, and churros.

Tortilla española is a delightful potato omelet, perfect for a hearty breakfast or weeknight dinner. Paella is a savory rice dish that invites family and friends to gather around a large pan, eat, and converse. Churros may have gained American fame from Disneyland, but they have been served in Spain for decades.

CHURROS

MAKES 6 CHURROS

3 tablespoons plus ½ cup (100 g) granulated sugar, divided

3 tablespoons plus 6 cups (1.4 kg) vegetable oil

1 cup (125 g) all-purpose flour

½ teaspoon salt

1 teaspoon ground cinnamon

1. Line a baking sheet with parchment paper. Line a large plate with paper towels.

2. In a medium saucepan, bring 1 cup (240 ml) of water, 3 tablespoons of the sugar, 3 tablespoons of the oil, the flour, and the salt, to a boil over medium heat. Remove the saucepan from the heat and stir in the flour. Let cool for 5 minutes.

3. Spoon the mixture into a piping bag fitted with a large star tip. Pipe 6-inch-long (15 cm) dough lines onto the prepared baking sheet and place in the freezer to set for 15 minutes.

4. In a large, deep, heavy pot, add the remaining 6 cups (1.4 kg) oil and heat to 375°F (190°C) over medium heat.

5. Add the remaining ½ cup (100 g) sugar and the cinnamon to a shallow dish.

6. Remove the dough from the freezer and carefully place 1 or 2 churros at time in the hot oil to cook for about 2 minutes, or until golden brown. Remove from the hot oil to the paper towel–lined plate to drain.

7. Working with one churro at a time, roll the cooked dough in the cinnamon sugar until coated. Serve immediately while warm.

BIG KIDS IN THE KITCHEN (7+)

Let your big kid roll the churros in cinnamon sugar (using tongs!). You can also put them in charge of dipping sauces, like chocolate, caramel, butterscotch, and peanut butter!

TORTILLA ESPAÑOLA

SERVES 4

2 tablespoons olive oil, divided

1 medium russet potato, peeled and thinly sliced

½ yellow onion, thinly sliced

6 large eggs

1 teaspoon salt

½ teaspoon ground black pepper

1. In a medium skillet, heat 1 tablespoon of the oil over medium heat. Add the potato and onion and cook for about 5 minutes, or until softened. Remove the pan from the heat.

2. In a large bowl, whisk together the eggs with the salt and pepper. Stir in the cooked potato and onion.

3. In the same skillet the potato and onion were cooked in, heat the remaining 1 tablespoon oil over medium heat. Pour the egg mixture into the pan and cook for 2 to 3 minutes, until the bottom is set. Slide a spatula around the edges to loosen and carefully flip the entire thing; cook 2 to 3 minutes more until the bottom has set.

4. Slide onto a plate, cut into wedges, and serve.

BIG KIDS IN THE KITCHEN (7+)

Big kids love to beat eggs! Give them a whisk (a small one is best!) and let them beat those eggs until light and fluffy.

PAELLA

SERVES 4

- 1 cup (240 ml) warm water
- 1 teaspoon saffron threads (see Tip)
- 2 tablespoons olive oil
- 1 white onion, diced
- 2 teaspoons minced garlic
- 1 red bell pepper, seeded and diced
- 1 green bell pepper, seeded and diced
- 2 cups (380 g) arborio rice
- 2½ cups (600 ml) chicken broth
- ¼ cup (35 g) frozen peas
- ¼ cup (30 g) fresh green beans
- ½ cup (70 g) sliced chorizo
- ½ pound (227 g) extra-large shrimp (16 to 20 count), peeled and deveined

1. Add the warm water and saffron threads to a small bowl and stir. Let soak for 10 minutes, then strain over a small bowl, discard the saffron threads, and set the liquid aside.

2. In a large skillet or wok, heat the oil over medium heat. Once shimmering, add the onion and garlic and cook for about 5 minutes, or until softened. Add the bell peppers and cook 2 minutes more.

3. Stir in the rice, chicken broth, and reserved saffron water. Bring to a boil, then reduce the heat to low and let simmer for 10 to 15 minutes, until the rice is almost done cooking.

4. Stir in the peas, green beans, chorizo, and shrimp. Cover and cook for 5 to 10 minutes, until the chorizo and shrimp are cooked through and the rice is tender. Serve immediately.

TIP

DID YOU KNOW **SAFFRON** IS ONE OF THE MOST **PRECIOUS** ITEMS ON EARTH? POUND FOR POUND, IT IS MORE EXPENSIVE THAN GOLD! LUCKY FOR US, SAFFRON THREADS ARE VERY **LIGHTWEIGHT**, SO A TEASPOON OF SAFFRON SHOULDN'T BREAK THE BANK. YOU CAN PURCHASE SAFFRON IN THE SPICE SECTION OF YOUR GROCERY STORE IN A STANDARD-SIZE CONTAINER, OR IF YOUR STORE HAS A **BULK SPICE SECTION**, OFTEN YOU CAN PURCHASE THE EXACT AMOUNT YOU NEED FOR A SINGLE RECIPE, SO NO SAFFRON GOES TO WASTE.

BUDDING SOUS-CHEFS (17+)

Paella is a dish that grows in flavor and depth by making it repeatedly and learning what needs tweaking and adjusting to make the perfect recipe worthy of your future generations. Let your sous-chef make the dish and give feedback on how to improve it next time.

SOUTH KOREA WEEK

(CHUSEOK, AUGUST 15)

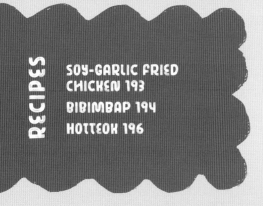

RECIPES

SOY-GARLIC FRIED
CHICKEN 193
BIBIMBAP 194
HOTTEOK 196

Globally, K-pop, K-dramas, and Korean cinema are incredibly popular, so it's no wonder that South Korean culture has made significant inroads into American life. Kimchi, once a niche ingredient, is now readily available in grocery stores.

This chapter offers recipes to introduce you to Korean flavors. However, for the full experience, consider dining at a local Korean restaurant to sample a wider range of dishes.

Korean Thanksgiving, or Chuseok, is a major holiday celebrated on the 15th day of the 8th lunar month. Like American and Canadian Thanksgiving, it's a time for family gatherings, feasting, and gratitude. However, Chuseok also involves unique traditions, such as visiting ancestral graves to pay respect, and offering memorial services.

SOY-GARLIC FRIED CHICKEN

SERVES 4

Fried Chicken

6 cups (1.4 L) vegetable oil, for frying

3 pounds (1.4 kg) boneless, skin-on chicken thighs, cut into 2-inch (5 cm) cubes

2 tablespoons rice wine vinegar

2 tablespoons minced fresh ginger

1 teaspoon salt

½ teaspoon ground black pepper

1 cup (130 g) cornstarch

Soy-Garlic Sauce

¼ cup (60 ml) soy sauce

¼ cup (60 ml) honey

2 tablespoons rice wine vinegar

2 teaspoons minced garlic

1 tablespoon sesame oil

1. Attach a deep-fry thermometer to the side of a large, deep, heavy pot. Add the vegetable oil and heat to 350°F (180°C) over medium heat.

2. Meanwhile, make the fried chicken: In a medium bowl, stir together the chicken pieces, vinegar, ginger, salt, and black pepper.

3. Add the cornstarch to a shallow bowl. Working with one piece of chicken at a time, remove a chicken piece from the wet mixture and allow any excess to drip off. Dredge the chicken piece through the cornstarch until coated evenly on all sides. Transfer to a plate.

4. Working in batches so as not to overcrowd the pot, add the chicken pieces to the preheated oil and cook for 1 to 2 minutes, then flip and cook for 2 to 3 minutes more, until crispy, golden, and cooked through. Transfer to a paper towel–lined plate.

5. To make the soy-garlic sauce: In a large bowl, whisk together the soy sauce, honey, vinegar, garlic, and sesame oil.

6. Add the fried chicken to the sauce and toss to coat. Serve immediately.

BIG KIDS IN THE KITCHEN (7+)

Not in the mood to make fried chicken? Head to your local grocery store deli or a fast-food joint and have your big kid order enough fried chicken for the whole family. Then, skip ahead to step 5.

BIBIMBAP

SERVES 4

Beef

½ cup (120 ml) soy sauce

2 tablespoons sesame oil

2 teaspoons minced garlic

2 teaspoons minced fresh ginger

½ pound (227 g) bottom round beef, thinly sliced

1 tablespoon vegetable oil

Gochujang Sauce

1 tablespoon gochujang

1 tablespoon soy sauce

1 teaspoon sesame oil

1 teaspoon rice vinegar

½ teaspoon minced garlic

1 teaspoon granulated sugar

Vegetables

2 cups (60 g) baby spinach

1 cup (150 g) julienne carrots

1 cup (145) sliced shiitake mushrooms

1 red bell pepper, seeded and sliced

Assembly

4 cups (660 g) cooked white rice

1 cup (90 g) bean sprouts

4 large eggs, fried

1 tablespoon white sesame seeds

1 tablespoon sliced green onions

1. To make the beef: In a medium bowl, whisk together the ½ cup (120 ml) soy sauce, 2 tablespoons sesame oil, 2 teaspoons minced garlic, and ginger. Add the beef to the bowl and toss to coat. Cover and marinate in the refrigerator for at least 1 hour and up to overnight.

2. In a medium skillet, heat the vegetable oil over medium heat. Once shimmering, add the beef, discarding the marinade, and cook, stirring often, for 3 to 5 minutes for medium well, or until it reaches desired doneness. Remove the pan from the heat.

3. To make the gochujang sauce: In a small bowl, whisk together the gochujang, 1 tablespoon soy sauce, 1 teaspoon sesame oil, vinegar, ½ teaspoon minced garlic, and sugar.

4. To steam the vegetables: Bring 1 inch (2.5 cm) of water to a boil in a large pot and place a steamer basket on top of the pot. Add the spinach, carrots, mushrooms, and bell pepper. Cover the pot and steam over medium-high heat for 5 to 7 minutes, until all the vegetables are tender.

5. To assemble: Divide the cooked rice among 4 bowls. Lay the spinach, bean sprouts, carrots, mushrooms, and peppers across the top of the rice. Pile the beef on top of the veggies, add 1 fried egg to each bowl, and drizzle with the gochujang sauce.

6. Sprinkle with the sesame seeds and green onions and serve.

BUDDING SOUS-CHEFS (17+)

Have your budding sous-chef thinly slice the beef. First place it in the freezer for about 30 minutes to harden slightly; this will help it not slip and slide around while they cut it.

HOTTEOK

MAKES 8 HOTTEOK

Dough

½ cup (120 ml) warm water (110°F, or 43°C)

1 tablespoon granulated sugar

1 teaspoon active dry yeast

1 cup (125 g) all-purpose flour, plus more for dusting

½ teaspoon salt

1 teaspoon vegetable oil

Nonstick cooking spray

Filling

½ cup (110 g) brown sugar

1 tablespoon ground cinnamon

¼ teaspoon ground nutmeg

1 tablespoon chopped peanuts

1 tablespoon chopped walnuts

1 tablespoon honey

Assembly

¼ cup (60 ml) vegetable oil, divided

¼ cup (60 ml) honey

1 tablespoon soy sauce

1. To make the dough: In a small bowl, stir together the warm water, granulated sugar, and yeast. Let it bloom for 5 minutes, or until frothy.

2. In a large bowl, using a hand or stand mixer, mix the flour and salt on low speed. Slowly pour in the yeast mixture and continue to mix on low until combined. Add the 1 teaspoon oil. Using the dough hook or your hands, knead the dough for 5 minutes, or until the dough is smooth and elastic. Form the dough into a tight ball, place it in a bowl greased with cooking spray and and cover with plastic wrap greased with cooking spray. Set the dough in a warm place to rise for about 1 hour, or until doubled in size.

3. Meanwhile, make the filling: In a small bowl, stir together the brown sugar, cinnamon, nutmeg, peanuts, walnuts, and honey.

4. Once the dough has risen, lightly flour a clean work surface. Turn out the dough onto it and cut 8 equal pieces, like a pizza. Working with one piece at a time, use a floured rolling pin to roll out each piece into a circle 3 to 4 inches (7.5 to 10 cm) in diameter.

5. Scoop 1 tablespoon of filling onto the center of a dough circle, then bring the edges of the dough up over the filling to meet one another; pinch together to seal the filling into the center of a ball. Gently press the ball back into a thick circle. Repeat with the remaining dough and filling.

6. To assemble: In a large skillet, heat 1 tablespoon of the vegetable oil over medium heat. Fry 2 or 3 hotteok at a time for 2 to 3 minutes per side, until golden and puffy. Add more oil to the pan as necessary.

7. In a small bowl, stir together the honey and soy sauce and then brush the mixture over the cooked hotteok. Serve immediately.

LITTLE HELPING HANDS (3+)

Your little helping hand will find brushing the glaze on top to be so fun. It's just like using a paintbrush!

JAPAN WEEK

(RESPECT FOR THE AGED DAY, SEPTEMBER 3)

Konnichiwa and Happy Japan Week!

While Japan may seem worlds away from the United States, we can still bridge the distance by exploring its rich culture and customs.

Respect for the Aged Day (Keiro no Hi), celebrated on the third Monday of September, is a beautiful example of Japanese values. This day is dedicated to honoring the elderly and recognizing their invaluable contributions to society. Let's celebrate by connecting with our own elders. Why not write a letter to your grandparents or a resident of a local nursing home? Their wisdom and experiences can teach us so much.

Japan's cultural heritage, from ancient traditions to cutting-edge technology, continues to inspire the world. Many of the electronic devices we use daily have their roots in Japanese innovation.

ONIGIRI

MAKES 8 ONIGIRI

¼ cup (40 g) finely chopped cooked or deli ham

2 tablespoons sesame seeds

4 cups (800 g) cooked short-grain rice, kept warm

2 sheets (7 by 8 inches, or 18 by 20 cm) nori (dried seaweed), cut into 8 (½ by 3-inch, or 1 by 7.5-cm) strips

1. In a large bowl, stir together the ham, sesame seeds, and rice. Divide the mixture into 8 equal portions and use wet hands to form into balls. Arrange on a serving plate.

2. Working with one ball at a time, wet your hands and shape and squeeze the ball into a triangle shape. Wrap the strip of nori around the bottom of each triangle.

3. Serve immediately and discard any leftovers.

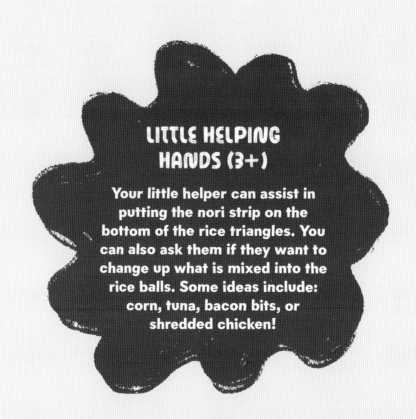

LITTLE HELPING HANDS (3+)

Your little helper can assist in putting the nori strip on the bottom of the rice triangles. You can also ask them if they want to change up what is mixed into the rice balls. Some ideas include: corn, tuna, bacon bits, or shredded chicken!

SUSHI ROLL

MAKES 2 ROLLS

1½ cups (250 g) cooked short-grain rice, kept warm

¼ cup (60 ml) rice vinegar

3 tablespoons granulated sugar

1 teaspoon salt

2 sheets nori (dried seaweed)

¼ cup (60 ml) Kewpie (Japanese) mayonnaise, divided

½ medium cucumber, sliced into matchsticks

1 medium avocado, pitted, peeled, and sliced

4 pieces imitation crab

2 tablespoons soy sauce, for serving

1. Wrap a sushi mat with plastic wrap.

2. In a large bowl, add the rice and stir to release some heat. Stir in the vinegar, sugar, and salt.

3. Lay a nori sheet onto the prepared sushi mat and, using wet hands, spread half of the rice evenly across the nori. Flip the nori over so the rice is facing down on the mat. Spread 2 tablespoons of the mayonnaise across the bottom inch (2.5 cm) in a line. Lay half of the cucumber, avocado, and crab sticks onto the mayonnaise.

4. Using the sushi mat, carefully roll up the sushi into a tight roll, making sure not to squeeze so hard that the filling comes out the sides. Release the roll from the plastic wrap and sushi mat. Wet a sharp knife with water and cut the roll into bite-size slices.

5. Repeat steps 3 and 4 with the remaining ingredients.

6. Pour the soy sauce into small dishes and use as a dip for the sushi roll slices. Serve immediately.

TWEENS ON THE SCENE (11+)

Making rice in a rice maker is easy and creates a consistent texture every time. Teach your tween how to use your rice maker: First, rinse the rice several times in a strainer, then place the rice in the rice maker. Pour water on top of the rice and select White Rice or press the "On" button. They will probably want to make rice any day as a snack!

INSTANT RAMEN (WITH A TWIST)

SERVES 1

1 package (3 ounces, or 85 g)
   instant ramen

1 large egg yolk

1 tablespoon Kewpie
   (Japanese) mayonnaise

1 soft-boiled egg

1 sheet nori (dried seaweed)

Sesame seeds, for garnishing

Sliced green onions, for
   garnishing

1. In a small saucepan, bring 3 cups (720 ml) of water to a boil over medium heat. Add the ramen noodles and cook for 3 minutes, or until soft. Remove the pan from the heat.

2. In a medium bowl, mix the seasoning mix from the ramen packet with the egg yolk and mayonnaise until well combined. Add about ½ cup (120 ml) of the noodle cooking water and whisk everything together.

3. Transfer the noodles to the bowl with the yolk mixture. Stir well to coat all the noodles with the sauce.

4. Slice the boiled egg in half and set it on top of the noodles. Add the sheet of nori, sprinkle with sesame seeds and green onions, and serve immediately.

BUDDING SOUS-CHEFS (17+)

Although many of these steps could be completed by a younger helper, teaching your budding sous-chef how to make this on their own will set them up for leaving home—as ramen is an inexpensive and easy meal to make. This hack will certainly impress their friends!

BRAZIL WEEK

(INDEPENDENCE DAY, SEPTEMBER 7)

Brazil is a huge country with diverse climates, geography, and cultures. Grab a Brazil travel guide from the library this week and try to discover differences and similarities among various regions across the country.

September 7, or Sete de Setembro, is a special day in Brazil, marking the country's Independence Day. In 1822, Brazil declared its independence from Portuguese colonial rule. Similar to Argentina's Spanish influence, Brazil's culture and language were shaped by Portuguese heritage. Today, Portuguese remains the official language.

Want to dive deeper into Brazilian culture? A churrascaria is a great place to start. These restaurants offer a unique dining experience, often featuring a lavish salad bar with Brazilian favorites like pão de queijo and feijoada. But the real showstopper is the meat! Gauchos, skilled chefs, roam the dining room, carving succulent cuts of meat directly onto your plate.

PÃO DE QUEIJO

MAKES 12 PIECES

1 cup (135 g) tapioca flour

½ cup (50 g) grated Parmesan cheese

¼ cup (30 g) cornstarch

1 teaspoon baking powder

¼ cup (60 ml) whole milk

¼ cup (½ stick, or 55 g) salted butter, melted

1 large egg

1. Preheat the oven to 400°F (200°C). Line a baking sheet with parchment paper.

2. In a large bowl, stir together the tapioca flour, Parmesan, cornstarch, and baking powder. While stirring, add the milk, melted butter, and egg and mix until everything is wet and combined.

3. Use a small cookie scoop to scoop the dough onto the prepared baking sheet, leaving about 1 inch (2.5 cm) of space between each piece. Bake for 20 to 25 minutes, until golden and cooked through. Serve warm.

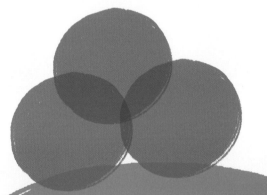

TWEENS ON THE SCENE (11+)

Have your tween scoop the dough onto the baking sheet using a cookie scoop. This is a helpful tool, and better than using a spoon, because it creates consistent scoops and the mixture will be easy to release.

BRIGADEIRO

MAKES 25 BRIGADEIRO

1 can (14 ounces, or 396 g) sweetened condensed milk

¼ cup (25 g) unsweetened cocoa powder

¼ cup (½ stick, or 55 g) butter

1 teaspoon vanilla extract

1 cup (192 g) sprinkles

25 mini paper baking liners

1. In a small saucepan, combine the sweetened condensed milk, cocoa powder, butter, and vanilla over medium heat and cook, stirring frequently, for 20 to 25 minutes, until the butter is melted and the mixture is thick and pulls away from the side of the pan.

2. Remove the pan from heat and let the mixture cool completely, about 1 hour.

3. Line a baking sheet with parchment paper.

4. Use a small cookie scoop to scoop about 25 balls of dough, then use your hands to form them into a tighter ball about 1 inch (2.5 cm) in diameter. Place the balls on the prepared baking sheet.

5. Place the sprinkles in a shallow bowl. Working one at a time, roll each ball in the sprinkles until evenly coated. Place the finished balls in mini paper baking liners and serve. Store at room temperature in an airtight container up to 3 days.

BIG KIDS IN THE KITCHEN (7+)

Your big kid can roll the brigadeiro in the sprinkles. In fact, if they would like to switch it up and roll them in something else—like mini chocolate chips, coconut, or rainbow sprinkles—let them do it!

KID-FRIENDLY CAIPIRINHA

SERVES 1

1 lime, cut into wedges

1 tablespoon simple syrup

1 cup (140 g) crushed ice

1 cup (240 ml) lemon-lime soda

1. In a glass, place the lime wedges and simple syrup and use a muddler or whisk to smush the limes down and mix with the syrup.

2. Add the crushed ice and pour in the lemon-lime soda. Stir gently to combine and serve immediately.

LITTLE HELPING HANDS (3+)

Your little helper can muddle the limes for you! Just tell them to go to town on smushing up those limes!

DUTCH OVEN WEEK

The term "Dutch oven" might be a bit misleading. While this cooking vessel may have a connection to Dutch traders who sold cast-iron pots in the American colonies, the essential characteristic of a Dutch oven is its versatility. It's a heavy-duty pot, often made of cast iron, with a tight-fitting lid that can withstand high temperatures, making it suitable for both stovetop and oven cooking.

If you don't have a traditional Dutch oven, don't worry! Many pots and pans can handle oven temperatures. Just check the manufacturer's guidelines to ensure they're safe for oven use. You can also use a baking dish for many of the recipes that call for a Dutch oven (so long as the recipe does not call for stovetop cooking).

One of the most fun ways to use a Dutch oven is over an open fire. Let the fire burn down to hot coals, then carefully place the Dutch oven among the coals. The lid helps to trap heat and moisture, creating a unique cooking environment similar to an oven.

NO-KNEAD BREAD

MAKES 1 LOAF

1½ cups (360 ml) warm water (120°F, or 50°C)

1 package (¼ ounce, or 7 g) active dry yeast

1 teaspoon salt

3¼ cups (440 g) bread flour

1. In the bowl of a stand mixer fitted with the paddle attachment, add the water, yeast, and salt and stir to combine. Let sit for 5 minutes to bloom.

2. Turn the mixer on low and, while mixing, add the flour, ½ cup (between 65 and 70 g) at a time, until it is all added. Once well combined, turn off the mixer, scrape down the sides of the bowl, and form the dough into a messy ball. Cover the bowl with a kitchen towel and let rise in a warm place for 2 to 3 hours, until doubled in size.

3. Place a Dutch oven with the lid on in the oven. Set the oven to 450°F (230°C).

4. Lightly flour a piece of parchment paper and lay it on a work surface. Turn out the dough onto the paper. Use your hands to form the dough into a "loaf" roughly the same size and shape as your Dutch oven. Use a bread lame or a sharp knife to slice a large X across the top of the loaf.

5. Carefully remove the hot Dutch oven from the oven and take off the lid. Lift up the parchment paper and set the loaf (parchment paper and all) into the Dutch oven, then place the lid back on.

6. Bake for 35 minutes, then remove the lid and bake for another 5 to 10 minutes to toast the top. Remove the pot from the oven and lift out the parchment paper to remove the loaf. Let cool for 1 hour on a wire cooling rack before slicing and serving.

BIG KIDS IN THE KITCHEN (7+)

Have your big kid add the flour to the mixer. Make sure they aim for the edges of the bowl and not the paddle.

BREAD PUDDING

SERVES 8

4 large eggs

3 cups (720 ml) whole milk

½ cup (100 g) granulated sugar

¼ cup (½ stick, or 55 g) butter, melted

1 teaspoon vanilla extract

½ teaspoon ground cinnamon

¼ teaspoon ground nutmeg

1 teaspoon salt

8 cups (280 g) cubed stale bread

1. Preheat the oven to 350°F (180°C).

2. In a large bowl, whisk together the eggs, milk, sugar, butter, vanilla, cinnamon, nutmeg, and salt. Add the bread and gently combine until evenly coated.

3. Scoop the mixture into a Dutch oven, cover, and bake for about 1 hour, or until cooked through. Let cool slightly and serve. Leftovers can be stored in the Dutch oven with the lid on in the refrigerator for up to 2 days.

BIG KIDS IN THE KITCHEN (7+)

Your big kid can stir the bread into the wet ingredients. Let them know that going slower with big swooping strokes is better than quick bursts of speed!

APPLE DUMP CAKE

SERVES 8

Nonstick cooking spray

2 cans (21 ounces, or 595 g, each) apple pie filling

1 box (15.25 ounces, or 432 g) yellow cake mix

½ cup (1 stick, or 115 g) butter, cubed

Ice cream or whipped cream, for serving

1. Preheat the oven to 350°F (180°C) and spray a large Dutch oven with nonstick cooking spray.

2. Pour the pie filling into the prepared Dutch oven and spread it across the bottom. Sprinkle the yellow cake mix evenly across the top of the pie filling. Place the butter cubes evenly across the dry cake mix. DO NOT STIR.

3. Place uncovered in the oven and bake for 40 to 50 minutes, until bubbling around the edges. Serve with ice cream or whipped cream.

TWEENS ON THE SCENE (11+)

Your tween can make this entire recipe themselves, start to finish! Just make sure they practice safety with the oven, and help them remove the hot cake from the oven when it's done cooking.

SOUTH AFRICA WEEK

(HERITAGE DAY, SEPTEMBER 24)

South Africa's Heritage Day is a vibrant celebration of the nation's rich cultural tapestry. It is a testament to the country's commitment to embracing diversity. Here are the many cultural groups that make up the Rainbow Nation:

- **ZULU.** Renowned for their intricate beadwork and powerful warrior traditions.

- **XHOSA.** Known for their vibrant Xhosa click language and their deep-rooted spiritual beliefs.

- **SOTHO.** With a strong emphasis on family and community, the Sotho people are known for their beautiful traditional attire.

- **TSWANA.** Celebrated for their intricate beadwork, pottery, and traditional dances.

- **VENDA.** A culture rich in oral traditions, music, and dance.

- **NDEBELE.** Known for their colorful and geometric wall paintings.

- **SWAZI.** A culture with a strong emphasis on tradition and respect for elders.

- **TSONGA.** Renowned for their intricate beadwork, pottery, and traditional dances.

- **AFRIKAANS:** A culture with strong Dutch and Huguenot influences, reflected in their language and cuisine.

AFRICAN GINGER BEER

SERVES 4

1 gallon (3.8 L) water

1 cup (200 g) granulated sugar

1 teaspoon dried ground ginger

½ teaspoon fresh lemon juice

¼ teaspoon citric acid

1 package (¼ ounce, or 7 g)
   active dry yeast

1. Clean and sterilize two 2-quart (2 L) jars with lids.

2. In a large pot, stir together the water, sugar, ginger, lemon juice, and citric acid over medium heat. Bring to a boil, then reduce the heat to low and let simmer for 5 minutes. Remove the pot from the heat and let cool completely to room temperature, about 1 hour.

3. Add the yeast and stir to dissolve completely. Divide the mixture evenly among the jars. Rest a lid on the top of each jar (do not screw them on!) and let ferment in a warm place for 2 to 3 days, until the bubbling has stopped.

4. At this point you can screw on the caps and refrigerate the jars for 1 more day before serving.

LITTLE HELPING HANDS (3+)

You can ask your little helpers to check on the jars each day to see if there are still bubbles popping up. They will love keeping an eye on the progress and will be excited to try the product!

KOEKSISTERS

MAKES 6 KOEKSISTERS

Syrup

2½ cups (500 g) granulated sugar

2 teaspoons fresh lemon juice

1 teaspoon vanilla extract

Dough

1½ cups (205 g) bread flour

4 teaspoons baking powder

¼ teaspoon salt

2 tablespoons cold salted butter, cubed

⅔ cup (165 ml) whole milk

6 cups (1.4 kg) vegetable oil, for frying

TWEENS ON THE SCENE (11+)

Tweens typically know how to braid at their age, and if not, this is a great time to teach them! If you don't know how to braid three strands, simply look up a tutorial online. It's easy!

1. To make the syrup: In a small saucepan, combine 1 cup (240 ml) of water with the sugar and stir. Bring to a boil over medium heat, and then boil for 7 minutes. Remove the pan from the heat stir in the lemon juice and vanilla. Let cool in the refrigerator.

2. To make the dough: In the bowl of a food processor, add the flour, baking powder, and salt and pulse to combine. Drop in the butter cubes and keep pulsing until crumbly. While the processor is running, gradually add the milk until the dough comes together in ball.

3. Lightly flour a clean work surface, then turn out the dough onto it. Use a floured rolling pin to roll out the dough to about ¼-inch (6 mm) thickness. Cut the dough into 18 strips about ½ inch (12 mm) thick and about 5 inches (12 cm) long. Take 3 strips, smoosh the tops together, and then braid the stands back and forth until you get to the end, pinching the end pieces together. Repeat with the remaining dough strips.

4. In a large, deep, heavy pot, heat the oil to 350°F (180°C) over medium heat. Slide 2 or 3 dough braids into the hot oil at a time and fry for 1 to 2 minutes per side, until golden and cooked through. Remove to a paper towel–lined plate.

5. Remove the pan of syrup from the fridge and place the cooked braids in the syrup in batches. Return the pan to the refrigerator and let the braids soak in the syrup for 3 minutes.

6. Use tongs to remove the braids from the syrup, then place them on a wire cooling rack to cool slightly. Serve warm.

BOBOTIE

SERVES 6

Nonstick cooking spray

1 pound (454 g) ground beef

1 cup (110 g) chopped yellow onion (about 1 medium onion)

2 teaspoons minced garlic

1 teaspoon ground turmeric

1 teaspoon curry powder

1 teaspoon salt

½ teaspoon ground coriander

½ teaspoon ground black pepper

1 large egg, beaten

½ cup (65 g) chopped dried apricots

¼ cup (35 g) raisins

½ cup (120 ml) whole milk

¼ cup (½ stick, or 55 g) salted butter, melted

1 large egg yolk

¼ teaspoon ground nutmeg

1. Preheat the oven to 350°F (180°C). Spray an 8 by 8-inch (20 by 20 cm) baking dish with nonstick cooking spray.

2. In a large skillet, brown the ground beef, while breaking it up with a wooden spoon, over medium heat, for 7 to10 minutes, until cooked through. Add the onion, garlic, turmeric, curry powder, salt, coriander, and pepper and cook, stirring often, for about 5 minutes, or until the onion is translucent. Transfer to a large heatproof bowl and let cool for about 20 minutes.

3. Stir the beaten egg, apricots, and raisins into the meat mixture, then spoon the mixture into the prepared baking dish.

4. Bake for 30 minutes, or until the egg sets.

5. Meanwhile, in a small bowl, whisk together the milk, butter, egg yolk, and nutmeg until combined.

6. Carefully remove the dish from the oven, pour the milk mixture over the top of the beef mixture, and return the dish to the oven. Bake for 15 minutes more. Remove from the oven and serve.

BIG KIDS IN THE KITCHEN (7+)

Your big kid can help make the milk and yolk topping by whisking the ingredients together and carefully pouring it over the meat!

GERMANY WEEK

(UNITY DAY, OCTOBER 3)

October 3 marks a significant moment in German history: German Unity Day. This holiday commemorates the reunification of East and West Germany in 1990, following the fall of the Berlin Wall the year before. While Germany's past is complex, the country has emerged as a vibrant and influential nation, learning from its history and embracing a hopeful future.

When you think of Germany, images of iconic symbols like lederhosen and cuckoo clocks, and hearty dishes like bratwurst and pretzels might come to mind. You might also associate Germany with the lively rhythms of polka music. These elements are all part of Germany's rich cultural heritage. Try looking up some polka music to accompany your Germany Week meal!

Another fun activity for this week is to look up photos of German castles. Sleeping Beauty Castle at Walt Disney World was designed after the Neuschwanstein Castle in Bavaria, Germany-- it is THAT magical! See what other beautiful ones you can find online or in a library book.

SOFT PRETZELS

MAKES 2 PRETZELS

2½ cups (360 ml) warm water (110°F, or 43°C)

1½ tablespoons dark molasses

1 package (¼ ounce, or 7 g) active dry yeast

3 tablespoons salted butter, softened

4 cups (500 g) all-purpose flour

½ teaspoon salt

2 tablespoons baking soda

2 tablespoons coarse salt

2 tablespoons salted butter, melted

Mustard, for dipping (optional)

BUDDING SOUS-CHEFS (17+)

Forming pretzels is the perfect task for a budding sous-chef. The trick is to hold up the dough when folding and then to set it on a flat surface for the final touches.

1. In a small bowl, stir together the warm water, the molasses, and yeast and let bloom for 5 minutes, or until foamy.

2. In a large bowl, using a hand or stand mixer, cream together the 3 tablespoons butter, flour, and salt on medium speed.

3. Use your hands or a stand mixer fitted with the dough hook attachment to knead the dough for 8 minutes, or until the dough is soft and elastic.

4. Turn out the dough out onto a lightly floured surface and cut into 2 equal pieces. Working with one piece at a time, slowly and carefully roll and pull the dough piece into a 2-foot-long (61 cm) rope about ¼ inch (6 mm) thick. Create a U shape by holding up each end, then cross the ends and bring them back down toward the bottom of the U. Pull the ends over to the sides of the pretzel, then pinch the ends onto the pretzel. Repeat with the remaining dough piece. Set each pretzel on a piece of parchment paper and cover with a clean towel to rest for 20 minutes.

5. Place a baking sheet upside down in the oven and set the oven to preheat to 500°F (260°C).

6. In a small pot, add 1 cup (240 ml) of water and the baking soda and stir over medium heat. Bring to a boil, then remove the pot from the heat. Brush the baking soda water onto each pretzel and sprinkle each one with the coarse salt.

7. Carefully slide each pretzel (with its parchment paper) onto the hot baking sheet in the oven. Bake for 10 to 15 minutes, until a deep-brown color.

8. Remove from the oven, brush with the melted butter, and serve immediately with mustard (if using).

SPETZI

SERVES 2

1 can (12 ounces, or 360 ml)
cola (such as Coca-Cola)

1 can (12 ounces, or 360 ml)
orange-flavored soda (such
as Fanta)

1. Divide the cola evenly between 2 glasses, then divide the orange soda between the glasses.

2. Stir gently with a spoon, top with ice, and serve immediately.

BIG KIDS IN THE KITCHEN (7+)

Your big kid can make this all themselves—just help them open the cans and place the glasses on paper towels to catch any spills!

LEBKUCHEN

MAKES 24 COOKIES

Cookies

½ cup (120 ml) honey

1 cup (220 g) brown sugar

¼ cup (½ stick, or 55 g) salted butter, softened

1 teaspoon baking powder

½ teaspoon baking soda

½ teaspoon salt

2 teaspoons ground cinnamon

½ teaspoon ground allspice

½ teaspoon ground ginger

¼ teaspoon ground cloves

¼ teaspoon ground nutmeg

1 large egg, beaten

1¾ cups (220 g) all-purpose flour, plus more for dusting

1 cup (115 g) almond flour

1 tablespoon fresh lemon juice

Nonstick cooking spray

Glaze

1 cup (125 g) confectioners' sugar

¼ cup (60 ml) fresh lemon juice (about 2 large lemons)

1 teaspoon vanilla extract

1. To make the cookies: In a large bowl, using a hand or stand mixer fitted with a paddle attachment, mix the honey, brown sugar, and butter on medium until combined, about 2 minutes. Add the baking powder, baking soda, salt, cinnamon, allspice, ginger, cloves, nutmeg, and egg and and mix for 2 more minutes.

2. Gradually add the all-purpose flour, followed by the almond flour, and continue mixing until a shaggy dough forms. Add 1 tablespoon lemon juice and mix until a soft ball forms. Place the dough in a large bowl greased with cooking spray, cover with a tea towel, and let rise in a warm place for 1 hour.

3. Preheat the oven to 350°F (180°C). Line two baking sheets with parchment paper.

4. Lightly flour a clean work surface, then turn out the dough onto it. Cut the dough in half. Working with one dough half at a time, roll out the dough to about ¾-inch (2 cm) thickness and use a 2- to 3-inch (5 to 7.5 cm) round biscuit or cookie cutter to cut the dough into 12 circles, placing them on the prepared baking sheets.

5. Bake for 10 to 12 minutes, one baking sheet at a time. Let rest for 5 minutes, then transfer the cookies to a wire cooling rack with a baking sheet under it.

6. Meanwhile, make the glaze: Mix the confectioners' sugar, ¼ cup (60 ml) lemon juice, and vanilla in a small bowl.

7. While the cookies are still warm, brush the tops with the glaze and let dry completely, about 20 minutes, before serving.

BIG KIDS IN THE KITCHEN (7+)

Ask your big kid to roll out the dough and cut it into circles.

CAMPFIRE WEEK

Does your family love the great outdoors? Camping is a fantastic way to bond with loved ones, unplug from technology, and create lasting memories. Whether you prefer the rustic charm of tent camping, the comfort of a camper, or the luxury of a cabin, there's a camping experience for almost everyone.

To enhance your camping adventure, try cooking delicious meals over an open fire. The recipes in this chapter are specifically designed for campfire cooking. Don't forget to gather sturdy roasting sticks and practice fire safety, especially with the little ones!

As the sun sets and the fire crackles, gather around the campfire to share stories and sing songs. Encourage family members to prepare a song or a tale to entertain everyone.

CAMPFIRE MEATBALL SUBS

MAKES 4 SUBS

20 frozen precooked Italian
meatballs, thawed

4 metal skewers

4 hot dog buns

2 cups (480 ml) marinara sauce,
warmed

2 cups (220 g) shredded
mozzarella cheese

1. Place 5 meatballs on each skewer. Cook over the campfire until the meatballs are warmed all the way through.

2. Use the hot dog buns to grab the meatballs and slide them off the skewers into the buns.

3. Spoon some sauce across the meatballs and sprinkle with the cheese while still hot. Serve immediately.

TWEENS ON THE SCENE (11+)

Your tween can help everyone get their meatballs nicely onto their skewers. Skewers with two prongs may be able to hold the meatballs a little more securely.

SAVORY S'MORES

MAKES 6 S'MORES

6 Babybel cheese rounds
  (0.71 ounce, or 20 g, each)

6 metal skewers

6 tablespoons strawberry jam

12 whole-grain wheat crackers

1. Remove and discard the outer coating from each cheese round. Thread 1 Babybel cheese onto a skewer and roast over the campfire until melty and warmed through.

2. Spread 1 tablespoon of the jam onto a cracker and place your melty cheese circle onto the jam. Use a second cracker to help slide the cheese off the skewer onto the cracker, press together like a sandwich, and serve immediately.

3. Repeat steps 1 and 2 with the remaining cheese, jam, and crackers.

LITTLE HELPING HANDS (3+)

This Savory S'more is really defined by what jam you put inside of it. Strawberry has a playful summer vibe, while fig jam heightens it to a more sophisticated flavor. Allow your little helper to choose the jam type and pack it for the campfire.

FOIL DINNER

SERVES 4

- 1 pound (454 g) ground beef
- 1 packet (2 ounces, or 57 g) onion soup mix
- 4 Yukon gold potatoes, peeled and sliced
- 2 cups (280 g) chopped carrots
- 1 cup (110 g) diced onion
- 2 tablespoons olive oil
- 1 teaspoon garlic powder
- 1 teaspoon salt
- ½ teaspoon ground black pepper
- ½ cup (120 ml) condensed cream of mushroom soup, divided

1. Prepare the foil dinners before leaving on your camping trip. In a large bowl, stir together the beef and onion soup mix, and divide into 4 equal portions. Form each into a ball, flatten into patties, and set on a plate.

2. In a second large bowl, combine the potatoes, carrots, onion, oil, garlic powder, salt, and pepper. Stir until the vegetables are well coated.

3. Lay out 4 pieces of aluminum foil (about 12 by 18 inches, or 30 by 46 cm). Scoop one-quarter of the vegetable mixture onto each foil piece, then lay 1 meat patty on top of the vegetables. Spoon 2 tablespoons of mushroom soup on top of each patty.

4. Seal the foil packet by bringing the sides together and folding over one another. Use a second piece of foil to double-wrap each packet to better secure the contents. Keep in a cooler with ice or ice packs until ready to use.

5. When you are at the campsite, allow the fire to die down to red-hot coals. Lay the foil dinners in the coals and let cook for about 15 to 30 minutes, until the beef is cooked all the way through (160°F, or 71°C).

6. Place each packet on a plate. Use tongs or oven mitts to carefully open. Let cool slightly, then mix up and serve.

BIG KIDS IN THE KITCHEN (7+)

If you own an infrared thermometer gun that can detect high temperatures, let your big kid check the campfire before you place the foil dinners in. The coals should be between 500 and 700°F (260 and 370°C).

FINGER FOOD WEEK

Eating with your hands can be a fun and engaging way to enjoy a meal, especially for young children. It can foster a sense of connection and togetherness as everyone partakes in the meal using their hands.

In many cultures around the world, eating with hands is a common practice. However, it's essential to be mindful of cultural norms and etiquette. Different cultures have specific customs for using certain hands (whether your right or left) to maintain hygiene and respect. If you're visiting a country where eating with your hands is customary, be sure to inquire about the appropriate etiquette.

The recipes in this section are perfect for enjoying with your hands. They also make excellent appetizers for parties, allowing guests to graze without the need for utensils.

FRUIT SKEWERS

MAKES 6 SKEWERS

1 pound (454 g) strawberries, stems removed

1 cup (145 g) jumbo blueberries

1 cantaloupe, rind and seeds removed, cut into ½-inch (12 mm) cubes

1 pound (454 g) large green grapes

1 cup (165 g) pineapple chunks

Fresh mint leaves, for garnishing (optional)

Optional Toppings

Chocolate sauce

Vanilla yogurt

1. Thread the fruit onto skewers, taking care to rotate placement among the strawberries, blueberries, cantaloupe, grapes, and pineapple.

2. If using, garnish with fresh mint and drizzle with chocolate sauce or yogurt.

BIG KIDS IN THE KITCHEN (7+)

Your big kid can certainly prep many of these fruits, especially the blueberries and grapes. Show them how to place them in a colander and wash the fruit before eating to make sure it is safe!

MINI QUESADILLAS

MAKES 6 QUESADILLAS

6 tablespoons salted butter, divided

1 package (12 count) "street taco" flour tortillas (4½ inches, or 11 cm)

3 cups (336 g) Mexican blend shredded cheese, divided

1. In a small skillet, melt 1 tablespoon of the butter over medium heat. Once bubbling, add a tortilla and sprinkle ½ cup (56 g) of the shredded cheese onto the tortilla. Place a second tortilla on top of the cheese.

2. Let cook for about 2 minutes, or until the cheese is melty and the underside is golden brown. Use a spatula to carefully flip over the quesadilla and cook for about 2 minutes more. Remove to a plate and cut into wedges.

3. Repeat steps 1 and 2 with the remaining ingredients.

LITTLE HELPING HANDS (3+)

Your little helper can decide what kind of dip options should be available for the family to dunk their quesadillas. Some ideas are salsa, sour cream, refried beans, or even ketchup!

PIGGIES IN A BLANKET

MAKES 24 PIGGIES

1 can (8 ounces, or 227 g) refrigerated crescent roll dough

1 package (12 ounces, or 340 g) beef cocktail sausages

¼ cup (½ stick, or 55 g) salted butter, melted

1 tablespoon white sesame seeds

Favorite condiments, for serving

1. Preheat the oven to 375°F (190°C). Line a large baking sheet with parchment paper.

2. Open the can of dough and roll it out in one piece on a clean work surface. Each crescent is perforated; use a knife to cut each perforated section into thirds, making a total of 24 dough pieces.

3. Working with one dough piece at a time, wrap 1 mini sausage in the dough piece, leaving the ends of the hot dog poking out. Repeat with the remaining dough and sausages, placing them all on the prepared baking sheet.

4. Brush all the dough with the melted butter and sprinkle with the sesame seeds.

5. Bake for 12 to 15 minutes, until the dough is cooked through and golden brown.

6. Serve with your favorite condiments.

TWEENS ON THE SCENE (11+)

Your tween can easily put this whole recipe together, just model to them how to wrap each of the piggies into the blankets and help them move the baking sheet in and out of the oven.

HALLOWEEN WEEK

(OCTOBER 31)

Boo! Happy Halloween! It's that magical time of year when kids dress up in costumes and go trick-or-treating. Whether you're into spooky haunts and ghostly tales or prefer the sweet side of Halloween, there's something for everyone to enjoy.

Halloween is also the perfect excuse to host a fun-filled party. The recipes in this chapter are perfect for a Halloween party or a small family gathering.

Coordinating costumes for the whole family to wear is so much fun! Some ideas for family costumes include everyone dressing as a different superhero (like Superman, Wonder Woman, Ironman); everyone dressing as a favorite book character (like Harry Potter, Waldo, Percy Jackson, Madeline.); or everyone dressing as the various jobs found in a restaurant (like a chef, pastry chef, server, host).

SPIDER DIP

SERVES 6

1 can (16 ounces, or 454 g) refried beans

1 package (8 ounces, or 227 g) cream cheese, softened

1½ cups (360 ml) sour cream, divided

1 packet (1 ounce, or 28 g) taco seasoning (or use the homemade taco seasoning on page 128)

1 cup (225 g) prepared guacamole

1 Roma tomato

1 bag (8.25 ounces, or 234 g) blue tortilla chips

1. In a medium bowl, stir together the refried beans and cream cheese and then spread into the bottom of a 9-inch (23 cm) pie plate.

2. In a small bowl, mix 1 cup (240 ml) of the sour cream with the taco seasoning and spread on top of the beans.

3. Spread the guacamole on top of the sour cream layer.

4. Put the remaining ½ cup (120 ml) sour cream into a piping bag (or use sour cream that comes in a squeeze container from the grocery store) and pipe a "spider web" of sour cream across the top of the guacamole. You can create this by making one straight line down the middle, followed by a perpendicular intersecting line, then straight lines through those to create 8 "pie pieces," and finally connect the lines to one another with a curve.

5. To make a "spider" out of the Roma tomato, cut one end off the tomato for the spider "body." Next, cut the other end off for the "head." Lastly, cut the remaining piece in half lengthwise, then cut each half into 4 slices for 8 "legs." Assemble the spider in the middle of the web on the dip.

6. Stick the blue tortilla chips around the outer edge of the dip and serve immediately.

BIG KIDS IN THE KITCHEN (7+)

Your big kid can help you smooth down each layer of the dip; simply hand them a rubber spatula and let them go to work!

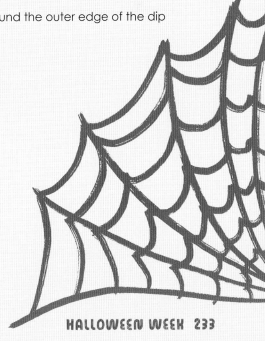

SCREAM CREAM BROWNIES

MAKES 12 BROWNIES

Brownie Layer
Nonstick cooking spray

2 large eggs

½ cup (120 ml) vegetable oil

1 teaspoon vanilla extract

1 cup (200 g) granulated sugar

½ cup (65 g) all-purpose flour

½ cup (70 g) dark cocoa powder

½ teaspoon salt

¼ teaspoon baking powder

Cream Cheese Layer
1 package (8 ounces, or 227 g) cream cheese, softened

¼ cup (50 g) granulated sugar

1 large egg

½ teaspoon vanilla extract

5 drops orange food coloring

For Serving
Whipped cream or ice cream

1. Preheat the oven to 350°F (180°C). Grease an 8 by 8-inch (20 by 20 cm) baking dish with nonstick cooking spray.

2. To make the brownie layer: In a large bowl, using a hand mixer or stand mixer, mix the 2 eggs, oil, and 1 teaspoon vanilla on low speed until combined. Continue mixing on low while adding the 1 cup (200 g) sugar, flour, cocoa powder, salt, and baking powder until all ingredients are combined.

3. Set aside ⅓ cup (80 ml) of the batter, then pour the rest into the prepared pan and spread evenly.

4. To make the cream cheese layer: Clean the mixer bowl, then add the cream cheese, ¼ cup (50 g) sugar, 1 egg, ½ teaspoon vanilla, and food coloring and mix on medium speed until smooth and creamy. Pour on top of the brownie batter and spread across it.

5. Dollop the reserved brownie batter on top of the cream cheese layer and use a toothpick or knife to "marble" the chocolate through with swirls.

6. Bake for 30 to 35 minutes, or until a toothpick inserted in the center comes out clean. Slice and serve with whipped cream or ice cream.

LITTLE HELPING HANDS (3+)

Your little helper can help you swirl the brownie and cream cheese layers together. To make it easier for them to hold, consider using a wooden skewer instead of a toothpick.

JACK-O'-PEPPERS

MAKES 6 PEPPERS

2 boneless chicken breasts (6 ounces, or 170 g, each)

1 cup (240 ml) favorite salsa

1 cup (165 g) diced tomatoes

1 packet (1 ounce, or 28 g) taco seasoning (or use the homemade taco seasoning on page 128)

Nonstick cooking spray

6 orange bell peppers

1 package (8.8 ounces, or 249 g) microwavable Mexican-style rice, prepared

1 can (15 ounces, or 425 g) black beans, rinsed and drained

2 cups (225 g) Mexican blend shredded cheese

1. In a slow cooker, place both chicken breasts, the salsa, diced tomatoes, and taco seasoning and stir. Let cook on low for 4 to 5 hours, until the internal temperature of the chicken reaches 165°F (75°C). Remove the chicken breasts and shred the meat. Return the shredded chicken to the slow cooker and stir everything together.

2. Preheat the oven to 350°F (180°C) and grease a 9 by 13-inch (23 by 33 cm) baking dish with nonstick cooking spray.

3. Carefully cut off the tops of the peppers to make a little cap, then hollow out the insides, removing all the seeds and white membrane. Use a knife to carve a little jack-o'-lantern face in one side of each pepper. Set the peppers in the pan, standing up, with the caps to the side for now.

4. In a large bowl, stir together the chicken, Mexican rice, black beans, and cheese. Scoop the filling into the peppers (leftovers can be served with the dinner in a bowl!) and set the pepper caps on top of the filling.

5. Bake for 20 to 30 minutes, until hot and the cheese is melty. Serve immediately.

BUDDING SOUS-CHEFS (17+)

Cutting the faces into the peppers is fun but can be challenging for little hands. Let your sous-chef step in and show off their creative side.

COZY SOUP WEEK

The Scandinavian concept of hygge, pronounced *hoo-gah*, embodies a sense of coziness, comfort, and contentment. Picture a warm blanket, a crackling fireplace, and a good book—that's hygge! And what better way to embrace hygge than with a bowl of comforting soup on a chilly fall day?

Soups are incredibly versatile. You can easily adjust the recipe to feed any number of people, and leftovers can be conveniently frozen and reheated. Pour the leftover soup into an airtight container and freeze solid. To loosen the frozen soup block, hold the closed container under hot water for a minute or two, then slide out the entire block into a large pot and reheat! Delicious fresh soup again.

As the colder months approach, let's embrace the hygge lifestyle and find joy in the simple pleasures. Don't let the cold weather dampen your spirits. Instead, focus on the cozy and comforting aspects of life that bring you happiness.

BROCCOLI CHEDDAR SOUP

SERVES 8

5 tablespoons salted butter, divided

½ cup (55 g) diced yellow onion

¼ cup (30 g) all-purpose flour

2 cups (480 ml) whole milk

2 cups (480 ml) chicken stock

1½ cups (235 g) frozen chopped broccoli

1 cup (140 g) diced carrots

¼ cup (25 g) diced celery

2½ cups (285 g) shredded sharp cheddar cheese

1 teaspoon salt

½ teaspoon ground black pepper

1. In a large skillet, melt 1 tablespoon of the butter over medium heat. Add the diced onion and cook, stirring occasionally, for about 5 minutes, or until translucent and soft.

2. In a large pot, melt the remaining 4 tablespoons butter over medium heat, then add the flour and cook, stirring constantly, for about 3 minutes, or until golden brown.

3. Slowly whisk in the milk and stock until combined, then bring to a boil. Reduce the heat to low and let simmer for 15 to 20 minutes, until creamy and thickened.

4. Add the broccoli, carrots, celery, and cooked onion and cook for an additional 10 to 15 minutes, until all the vegetables are soft.

5. Stir in the cheddar cheese and cook for 1 to 2 minutes more, until the cheese is melted. Season with salt and pepper and serve immediately.

TWEENS ON THE SCENE (11+)

Your tween can add the veggies to the soup and stir them in. If you purchase pre-cut vegetables at the grocery store, it cuts down on the prep time and allows your tween to do more!

TOMATO SOUP

SERVES 6

4 cups (720 g) diced fresh Roma tomatoes

½ cup (55 g) diced white onion

4 teaspoons minced garlic

2 cups (480 ml) chicken broth

2 tablespoons salted butter

2 tablespoons all-purpose flour

2 teaspoons salt

2 teaspoons granulated sugar

1 tablespoon Italian seasoning

1. In a large pot, add the tomatoes, onion, garlic, and broth and cook over medium heat for 20 minutes.

2. Use an immersion blender to carefully puree the mixture in the large pot and remove the pot from the heat.

3. In a separate large pot, melt the butter over medium heat, then add the flour. Cook, stirring constantly, for 4 minutes to make a roux. Add the tomato puree to the roux, one ladle at a time, while whisking.

4. Add the salt, sugar, and Italian seasoning, adjusting the seasoning to taste, and stir to combine.

5. Serve immediately or store in an airtight container in the refrigerator up to 5 days.

BUDDING SOUS-CHEFS (17+)

Using an immersion blender can be quite tricky. It has blades on the bottom that spin and puree the food, but it also utilizes suction to draw the food into the blades. It requires a firm hand! Be sure to wear an apron in case it (literally) backfires!

FRENCH ONION SOUP

SERVES 2

1 tablespoon salted butter

1 tablespoon olive oil

2 cups (220 g) diced yellow onion

2½ cups (20 ounces, or 600 ml) beef broth

1 tablespoon cooking sherry

1 teaspoon dried thyme

½ teaspoon ground black pepper

2 slices whole wheat bread

1 cup (110 g) shredded Gruyère cheese, divided

Fresh thyme leaves, for garnishing

1. In a large pot, add the butter and olive oil over medium heat. Once the butter is melted, add the onion and cook for 2 minutes, or until translucent and soft.

2. Stir in the broth, sherry, dried thyme, and pepper. Bring to a boil, then reduce the heat to low and let simmer for 30 minutes.

3. Place the oven rack at the top and preheat the broiler to high.

4. Remove the pot from the stovetop and pour the soup through a fine-mesh strainer into four oven-proof bowls. Place a slice of bread on top of the soup in each bowl and sprinkle each bread slice with ½ cup (55 g) shredded cheese.

5. Place the bowls on a baking sheet and broil in the oven for 30 seconds, or just until the cheese is melted but not burnt. Sprinkle each bowl with fresh thyme and serve immediately.

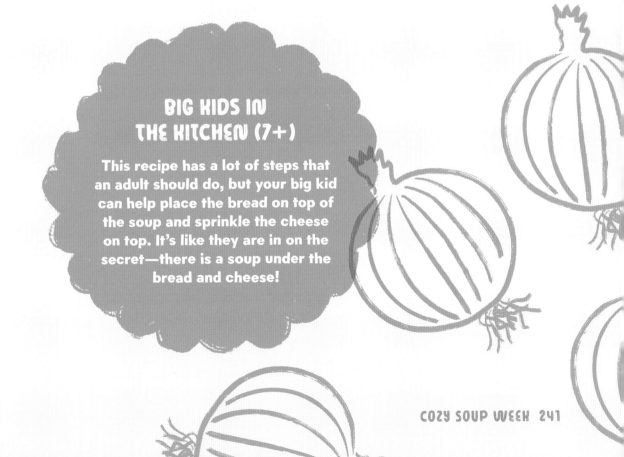

BIG KIDS IN THE KITCHEN (7+)

This recipe has a lot of steps that an adult should do, but your big kid can help place the bread on top of the soup and sprinkle the cheese on top. It's like they are in on the secret—there is a soup under the bread and cheese!

BREAKFAST WEEK

While breakfast is a daily ritual, many of us rush through it, opting for quick and convenient options like cereal, oatmeal, or a simple beverage. To savor the breakfast experience and enjoy a more substantial meal, consider dedicating a dinnertime to breakfast foods. This allows for extra preparation time and a leisurely meal.

Breakfast traditions vary widely across the globe, from pancakes to savory dishes like meat and fish. The recipes in this chapter may be familiar or entirely new, depending on your cultural background.

To complete your breakfast menu, pair these dishes with freshly squeezed juice or a side of fresh fruit for a balanced and nutritious meal.

HASH YAMS

SERVES 4

2 large sweet potatoes, peeled and shredded

2 large eggs

1 teaspoon salt

½ teaspoon ground black pepper

Nonstick cooking spray

1. In a large bowl, mix the sweet potato, egg, salt, and pepper until well combined.

2. Grease a medium skillet with nonstick cooking spray and place over medium heat.

3. Scoop the potato mixture into the pan and smooth out to evenly fill the pan. Let cook, without stirring, for 3 to 5 minutes, until the underside is browned. Carefully flip the whole patty over and cook the other side 3 to 5 minutes more, until everything is crispy and slightly golden brown. Serve immediately.

TWEENS ON THE SCENE (11+)

This is a dish your tween could learn to master on their own, especially if they have help prepping the potatoes. Using a spinning grater will make it much easier than a box grater!

SHEET PAN PANCAKES

SERVES 10

Nonstick cooking spray

3 cups (375 g) all-purpose flour

2 tablespoons baking powder

2 tablespoons granulated sugar

½ teaspoon salt

2½ cups (600 ml) whole milk

2 large eggs

½ cup (1 stick, or 115 g) butter, melted

1 cup (145 g) strawberries, hulled and sliced

1 cup (145 g) blueberries

Maple syrup, for serving

1. Preheat the oven to 425°F (220°C). Grease a rimmed half sheet pan with nonstick cooking spray.

2. In a large bowl, combine the flour, baking powder, sugar, and salt. Add the milk, eggs, and melted butter and mix until the batter is wet and has no flour pockets. Pour the batter into the prepared baking sheet.

3. Distribute the strawberries and blueberries across the top of the batter and push them down slightly into the batter.

4. Bake for 15 to 20 minutes, until a toothpick inserted in the center comes out clean.

5. Cut into squares and serve with maple syrup.

LITTLE HELPING HANDS (3+)

Have your little helper sprinkle on and press the fruit into the batter. It doesn't matter if it isn't perfect!

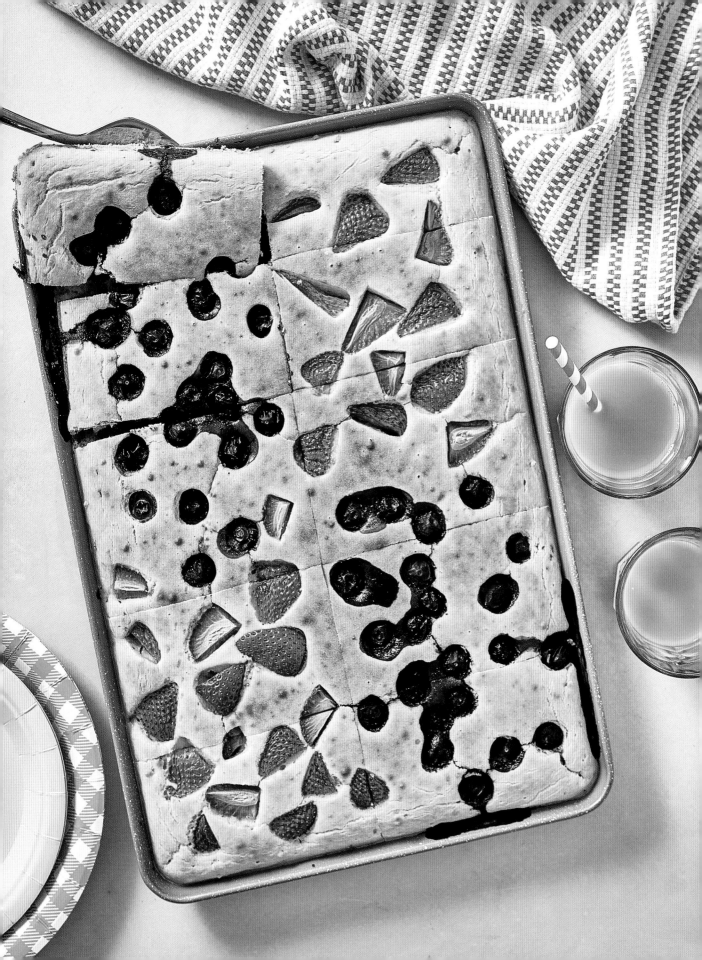

OVEN OMELETS

SERVES 9

Nonstick cooking spray

8 large eggs

1 cup (240 ml) whole milk

½ teaspoon salt

½ teaspoon ground black pepper

6 ounces (170 g) diced cooked or deli ham

½ cup (55 g) shredded cheddar cheese

½ cup (55 g) diced onion

½ cup (75 g) diced bell pepper

1. Preheat the oven to 350°F (180°C). Grease an 8 by 8-inch (20 by 20 cm) dish with nonstick cooking spray.

2. In a medium bowl, add the eggs, milk, salt, and black pepper and whisk until fully combined. Add the ham, cheese, onion, and bell pepper and stir to incorporate. Pour the egg mixture into the prepared dish.

3. Bake for 45 to 50 minutes, until the middle is firm when shaken.

4. Cut into squares and serve immediately.

BIG KIDS IN THE KITCHEN (7+)

Remember the hack to crack eggs easily? Just hold the egg about six inches above the countertop and just drop it—the egg will crack but not explode and allow you to carefully separate both shell halves from the egg! Even your big kid can do this!

US THANKSGIVING WEEK

Happy Thanksgiving! It's a time for reflection, gratitude, and gathering with loved ones. Traditionally celebrated with a feast featuring turkey, mashed potatoes, gravy, stuffing, and pumpkin pie, Thanksgiving offers an opportunity to connect with family and friends.

While these classic dishes are beloved, don't feel confined to tradition. Thanksgiving is a perfect time to experiment with new flavors and cuisines. Consider inviting friends and neighbors from diverse backgrounds to share their culinary traditions. This not only adds variety to the meal but also fosters cultural exchange and appreciation.

Let's embrace the spirit of Thanksgiving by giving thanks for the abundance in our lives and sharing it with others.

MASHED POTATOES

SERVES 8

8 large Yukon gold potatoes, peeled and cubed

½ cup (1 stick, or 115 g) salted butter, cut into slices

½ cup (120 ml) heavy whipping cream

1 tablespoon garlic powder

1 tablespoon Italian seasoning

1 tablespoon salt

1 teaspoon ground black pepper

Gravy, for serving (optional)

1. Fill a large pot two-thirds full of water and bring to a boil over medium heat. Add the potatoes and cook, uncovered, for 15 to 25 minutes, until the potatoes are fork-tender. Drain in a colander and return the potatoes to the pot.

2. Add the butter to the pot and begin to mash the potatoes with a potato masher. Once the butter has melted, pour in the cream and continue to mash until everything is nice and smooth.

3. Add the garlic powder, Italian seasoning, salt, and pepper and stir to combine. Serve hot with gravy (if using).

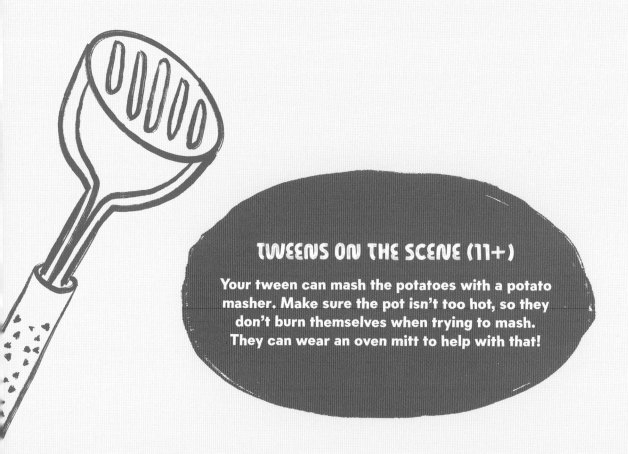

TWEENS ON THE SCENE (11+)

Your tween can mash the potatoes with a potato masher. Make sure the pot isn't too hot, so they don't burn themselves when trying to mash. They can wear an oven mitt to help with that!

STUFFING

SERVES 6

½ loaf sliced whole wheat bread, broken into pieces

½ loaf sliced white bread, broken into pieces

6 pork sausage links

1 cup (2 sticks, or 230 g) salted butter

2 ribs celery, diced

1 Granny Smith apple, cored and diced

2 tablespoons dried parsley

1 tablespoon ground sage

1 tablespoon dried rosemary

2 tablespoons dried thyme

1 tablespoon salt

1 teaspoon ground black pepper

1. Add the bread pieces to a large pot or bowl.

2. In a large skillet, cook the sausage links over medium heat for 5 to 8 minutes, until cooked through. Transfer to a paper towel–lined plate. Once slightly cooled, cut the links into bite-size pieces and sprinkle into the bread.

3. In the same skillet (with the sausage grease still in it), melt the butter over medium heat. Add the celery and cook 2 minutes, until softened. Pour the celery and butter over the bread and sausage and toss to coat. Add the diced apple.

4. Season the bread mixture with the parsley, sage, rosemary, thyme, salt, and pepper and toss to coat.

5. Scoop the bread mixture into an oven-proof dish and bake at 350°F (180°C) for 20 to 30 minutes, until warmed through. Serve with Thanksgiving dinner or enjoy any day.

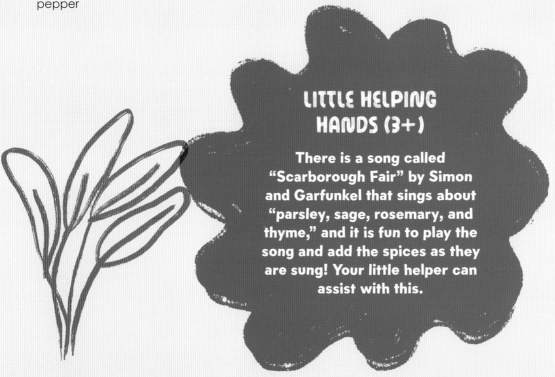

LITTLE HELPING HANDS (3+)

There is a song called "Scarborough Fair" by Simon and Garfunkel that sings about "parsley, sage, rosemary, and thyme," and it is fun to play the song and add the spices as they are sung! Your little helper can assist with this.

TURKEY BREAST TENDERLOINS

SERVES 6

2 tablespoons olive oil

2 tablespoons apple cider vinegar

1 tablespoon light brown sugar

2 teaspoons minced garlic

1 teaspoon dried thyme

1 teaspoon dried oregano

½ teaspoon paprika

1 teaspoon salt

¼ teaspoon ground black pepper

1 package (24 ounces, or 680 g) turkey breast tenderloins

Nonstick cooking spray

Mashed Potatoes (page 248), for serving (optional)

Stuffing (page 250), for serving (optional)

1. In a large bowl, stir together the oil, vinegar, brown sugar, garlic, thyme, oregano, paprika, salt, and pepper.

2. Add the turkey tenderloins to the bowl and toss to coat. Cover with plastic wrap and let marinate in the refrigerator for at least 1 hour and up to overnight.

3. Preheat the oven to 350°F (180°C). Grease a 9 by 13-inch (23 by 33 cm) baking dish with nonstick cooking spray.

4. Place the turkey medallions, rounded sides up, in the prepared baking dish. Bake for 60 to 70 minutes, until the internal temperature reaches 165°F (75°C). Remove from the oven and let the turkey sit in the pan for 5 to 10 minutes to retain its juices.

5. If using, serve with mashed potatoes and stuffing.

TWEENS ON THE SCENE (11+)

This is a great recipe for your tween to prepare on their own. It is a staple main dish, and they will be very proud to do it on their own! If the turkey comes seasoned, it is even easier! Just skip the marinade steps and go straight to baking.

VEGGIE WEEK

Are you a vegetarian? Whether you are or aren't, we all need to incorporate plenty of vegetables into our diets. Vegetables offer a wealth of health benefits, including boosting our vitamin intake, lowering the risk of disease, improving digestion, enhancing immune function, and lowering blood pressure. So, if we should be eating vegetables, let's make them delicious!

There are countless ways to enjoy veggies. You can sauté them in oil or butter, roast them in the oven, or eat them raw with a dip. The key is to find preparation methods that your family loves, ensuring that vegetables become a regular part of your meals.

Many recipes in this book, beyond this chapter, are either vegetarian or include a generous amount of vegetables. So, if you're a vegetarian or preparing a meal for one, simply browse through the pages and you'll find plenty of tasty options!

BLACK BEAN HUMMUS

SERVES 6

1 teaspoon minced garlic

1 can (15 ounces, or 425 g) black beans, rinsed and drained

2 tablespoons fresh lime juice

1½ tablespoons tahini

1 teaspoon ground cumin

1 teaspoon salt

½ teaspoon paprika

Fresh cilantro leaves

Favorite vegetables (such as baby carrots, cucumber slices, bell pepper slices, broccoli florets, cauliflower florets, radish slices), for serving

1. In a blender or food processor, process the garlic, beans, lime juice, tahini, cumin, salt, and paprika until smooth.

2. Transfer to a serving bowl, sprinkle with cilantro, and serve with your favorite vegetables.

LITTLE HELPING HANDS (3+)

A little helper can make this hummus all by themselves if you prep the ingredients first. Just get everything ready and they can add the items to the blender and press the blender buttons. They can also choose which veggies to serve with the dip!

VEGGIE BURGERS

MAKES 6 BURGERS

1 can (15 ounces, or 425 g) black beans, rinsed and drained

½ cup (55 g) diced onion

¼ cup (20 g) old-fashioned oats

¼ cup (70 g) diced carrot

2 tablespoons olive oil

1 teaspoon minced garlic

1 teaspoon salt

½ teaspoon ground black pepper

1 cup (100 g) plain dried bread crumbs

Nonstick cooking spray

6 hamburger buns

6 slices cheddar cheese

6 leaves butter lettuce

Favorite condiments, for serving

1. Line a baking sheet with parchment paper.

2. In a food processor or blender, process the black beans, onion, oats, carrot, oil, garlic, salt, and pepper until all the ingredients come together in a thick paste. Divide the mixture into 6 portions and use your hands to form into 3-inch-thick (7.5 cm) patties.

3. Add the bread crumbs to a shallow bowl. Press one side of each patty into the bread crumbs, flip, and press again. Set on the prepared baking sheet.

4. Heat a large skillet over medium heat and coat with nonstick cooking spray. Working in batches, add the patties and cook for about 5 minutes, or until crispy and browned. Flip and cook for 5 minutes more, or until evenly cooked. Add a slice of cheese to each burger and cook until the cheese is just melted, 1 to 2 minutes. Transfer to a paper towel–lined plate.

5. Place the cooked patties on the bottom halves of the buns, cover each one with a slice of cheese, and top with lettuce. Serve immediately with your favorite condiments.

BUDDING SOUS-CHEFS (17+)

Working with the patty mixture can be a little tricky, but your budding sous-chef can handle it. I recommend wearing food-prep gloves when forming the patties with your hands to make less mess.

ZUCCHINI BREAD

SERVES 12

Nonstick cooking spray

3 cups (375 g) all-purpose flour

1 teaspoon salt

1 teaspoon baking powder

1 teaspoon baking soda

1 tablespoon ground cinnamon

3 large eggs

1 cup (240 ml) vegetable oil

1 tablespoon vanilla extract

2 cups (280 g) peeled and grated zucchini (about 2 medium zucchini)

1. Preheat the oven to 325°F (170°C). Grease two 1-pound (454 g) loaf pans with nonstick cooking spray.

2. In a large bowl, mix the flour, salt, baking powder, baking soda, and cinnamon. Add the eggs, oil, and vanilla and mix to combine. Fold in the zucchini until everything is wet. Divide the batter between the two prepared pans.

3. Bake for 55 to 60 minutes, until a toothpick inserted in the center comes out clean.

4. Let cool in the pans for at least 20 minutes, then remove from the pans, and slice to serve. Store leftovers keep in a zip-top plastic bag at room temperature up to 3 days.

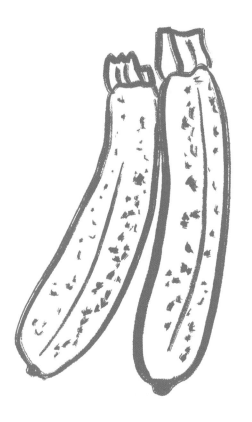

BIG KIDS IN THE KITCHEN (7+)

If you have a rotary grater, your big kid can help you to prepare the zucchini. A rotary grater keeps little fingers away from any sharp edges and creates a nice uniform cut every time.

HANUKKAH WEEK

Hanukkah, also known as the Festival of Lights, is an eight-day Jewish celebration that can occur between November 28 and December 27, starting on the 25th day of Kislev of the Hebrew calendar. It commemorates the rededication of the Holy Temple in Jerusalem. Here are some key Hanukkah traditions:

• **MENORAH LIGHTING.** Each night, a candle is lit on the menorah, symbolizing the miracle of the oil that lasted for eight days.

• **TRADITIONAL FOODS.** Hanukkah is associated with fried foods like latkes (potato pancakes) and sufganiyot (jelly doughnuts).

• **DREIDEL SPINNING.** A fun game involving a four-sided spinning top, called a dreidel, with Hebrew letters. Dreidels can be purchased at many stores or online. Here's how you play:

1. **SET-UP.** Each player starts with an equal number of "bets" (like coins or candies).

2. **SPINNING.** Players take turns spinning the dreidel.

3. **INTERPRETING THE RESULTS.** Nun (נ), nothing happens; Gimel (ג), the player takes the entire pot; Hey (ה), the player takes half the pot; Shin (ש), the player puts one bet into the pot.

4. **CONTINUE PLAYING:** The game continues until one player has all the bets.

LATKES

MAKES 6 LATKES

½ cup (120 ml) vegetable oil, for frying

2 large russet potatoes, peeled and grated

1 small yellow onion, grated

1 large egg

1 tablespoon all-purpose flour

½ teaspoon salt

¼ teaspoon ground black pepper

Applesauce, for serving

Sour cream, for serving

1. In a large, deep, heavy skillet or Dutch oven, heat the oil to 350°F (180°C) over medium heat.

2. In a large bowl, add the potato and onion. Use a paper towel to press down on the shreds to release excess liquid. Carefully drain the liquid from the bowl.

3. Add the egg, flour, salt, and pepper to the bowl and stir until well combined.

4. Scoop out 2-tablespoon portions of the potato mixture and flatten them in your hands to form disks.

5. Place the disks directly into the hot oil, working in batches, and fry for 2 to 3 minutes per side, until browned and crispy. Transfer to a paper towel–lined plate.

6. Serve warm with applesauce and sour cream.

TWEENS ON THE SCENE (11+)

If you have a rotary grater, your tween can grate all the potatoes and onion with ease. Make sure the grater is firmly suctioned to the counter or tabletop so it doesn't go flying when the grating begins!

EGG CREAM

MAKES 1 DRINK

3 tablespoons chocolate syrup

¼ cup (60 ml) whole milk

¾ cup (180 ml) plain seltzer water

1. Add the chocolate syrup and milk to a glass or cup and stir well to combine.

2. Pour in the seltzer and stir quickly to create a froth. Serve immediately.

BIG KIDS IN THE KITCHEN (7+)

Even a 7-year-old can make this drink! Just help them measure the chocolate syrup so they don't go overboard!

BLACK AND WHITE COOKIES

MAKES 9 COOKIES

Cookies

⅓ cup (75 g) salted butter, softened

½ cup (100 g) granulated sugar

1 large egg

1 ¼ cups (155 g) all-purpose flour

½ teaspoon baking powder

½ teaspoon salt

½ teaspoon vanilla extract

½ teaspoon lemon extract

⅓ cup (75 ml) whole milk

Glazes

2½ cups (313 g) confectioners' sugar

4 tablespoons whole milk, divided

¼ teaspoon vanilla extract

¼ cup (25 g) unsweetened cocoa powder

1. Preheat the oven to 375°F (190°C). Line a baking sheet with parchment paper.

2. To make the cookies: In a large bowl, using a hand or stand mixer fitted with the paddle attachment, cream together the butter and sugar on medium speed for 2 minutes, then add the egg and mix for 1 minute.

3. While the mixer is running on low speed, add the flour, baking powder, and salt and mix to combine. Add the ½ teaspoon vanilla extract and lemon extract, then drizzle in the ⅓ cup (75 ml) milk. Keep mixing until everything comes together as a dough.

4. Use a 3-tablespoon cookie scoop to scoop the dough onto the prepared baking sheet, evenly spread apart. Bake for 12 to 15 minutes, until a toothpick inserted in the center of a cookie comes out clean. Let the cookies cool completely on the sheet, about 45 minutes.

5. Meanwhile, make the glazes: In a medium bowl, combine the confectioners' sugar and 3 tablespoons of the milk and whisk until smooth. Pour half of the mixture into a second medium bowl.

6. To the first bowl, add the ¼ teaspoon vanilla and stir. To the second bowl, add the cocoa powder and the remaining 1 tablespoon milk and stir until smooth.

7. Once the cookies are completely cooled, place them on a wire cooling rack over a baking sheet. Use a spoon to carefully glaze one half of each cookie with vanilla glaze and let dry for about 10 minutes. Then, glaze the other half with the chocolate glaze and let dry an additional 10 minutes before serving.

TWEENS ON THE SCENE (11+)

Have your tween take charge of the glazing.

CHRISTMAS WEEK

(DECEMBER 25)

Christmas is a beloved holiday celebrated worldwide, marked by festive traditions like decorating Christmas trees, exchanging gifts, and enjoying delicious food. While the commercial aspects of the season can be overwhelming, it's important to remember the heart of Christmas: family, friends, and the joy of giving.

Involving your family in the kitchen can create cherished memories. Baking cookies, preparing festive meals, and sharing in the culinary experience can bring everyone together. Don't be afraid to experiment with new recipes and flavors, and consider sharing your homemade treats with neighbors and friends.

Whether you celebrate Christmas for religious reasons or simply enjoy the festive atmosphere, the spirit of the season can be shared by all. Embrace the joy, kindness, and togetherness that Christmas brings.

GINGERBREAD COOKIES

MAKES 12 COOKIES

½ cup (1 stick, or 115 g) salted butter

½ cup (110 g) brown sugar

3 tablespoons molasses

1¾ cups (220 g) all-purpose flour

1 tablespoon ground ginger

1 teaspoon ground cinnamon

½ teaspoon baking soda

2 tablespoons half-and-half

1 container (16 ounces, or 454 g) white frosting.

1. In a large bowl using a hand or stand mixer, mix the butter and brown sugar on medium speed for 1 to 2 minutes, until creamy. Add the molasses, then gradually add the flour as you continue to mix on low speed.

2. Add the ginger, cinnamon, baking soda, and half-and-half to the bowl and mix until everything comes together as a dough.

3. Turn the dough out onto a sheet of plastic wrap and flatten it into a disk about ½ inch (12 mm) thick. Place it in the refrigerator to chill for 1 hour.

4. Preheat the oven to 375°F (190°C). Line a baking sheet with parchment paper.

5. Lay a large sheet of parchment paper on the counter. Place the unwrapped dough onto the paper and lay another sheet of parchment paper on top of the disk. Use a rolling pin to flatten the dough into about ¼-inch (6 mm) thickness.

6. Choose whatever cookie cutters you want and press shapes out of the dough. Move the completed shapes to the prepared baking Re-roll the dough scraps and cut out more shapes.

7. Bake for 10 to 12 minutes, until the bottoms are browned and the tops are no longer puffy. Let the cookies to cool on the baking sheet for about 30 minutes.

8. Once the cookies are completely cooled, spread frosting over the tops of the cookies or use it to create fun designs.

LITTLE HELPING HANDS (3+)

Let little helpers select the cookie cutters. Any shape is fine! They can also decorate their own cookies with frosting.

FESTIVE PUNCH

SERVES 6

3 cups (720 ml) cold water

¾ cup (150 g) granulated sugar

5 cinnamon sticks

1 bottle (24.5 ounces, or 725 ml) sparkling red grape juice, chilled

1 cup (240 ml) orange juice, chilled

½ cup (120 ml) fresh lemon juice (about 4 large lemons), chilled

6 cups (1.4 L) lemon-lime soda, chilled

Ice

2 large oranges, sliced

2 large lemons, sliced

2 large limes, sliced

1. In a medium saucepan, stir together the cold water with the sugar and cinnamon sticks and bring to a boil over medium heat. Reduce the heat to low and let simmer for 5 minutes. Remove from the heat and refrigerate to chill completely, about 1 hour.

2. When you are ready to serve the punch, pour the chilled cinnamon syrup into a large punch bowl, then add the sparkling grape juice, orange juice, lemon juice, and lemon-lime soda and stir gently to combine.

3. Add ice and float the orange, lemon, and lime slices on top as decoration.

BUDDING SOUS-CHEFS (17+)

Ask your sous-chef to make this for your next holiday party, and maybe they will even like to serve it up when guests come over!

CHRISTMAS WREATH DOUGHNUTS

MAKES 6 DOUGHNUTS

Doughnuts

Nonstick cooking spray

1 box (15.25 ounces, or 432 g) red velvet cake mix

½ cup (120 ml) vegetable oil

3 large eggs

Buttercream Frosting

½ cup (1 stick, or 115 g) salted butter, softened

2 teaspoons vanilla extract

2 cups (250 g) confectioners' sugar

1 tablespoon whole milk

5 drops green food coloring

Assembly

2 tablespoons assorted red and green sprinkles

1. Preheat the oven to 350°F (180°C). Grease a 6-divot doughnut pan with nonstick cooking spray.

2. To make the doughnuts: In the bowl of a stand mixer fitted with the paddle attachment, add the cake mix, 1 cup (240 ml) of water, the oil, and eggs and mix until everything is wet.

3. Scoop the batter into a piping bag, then pipe the dough into the prepared divots until each one is two-thirds full. Discard any excess batter.

4. Bake for 15 to 18 minutes, or until a toothpick inserted into the center of a doughnut comes out clean. Let the doughnuts cool in the pan for 10 minutes. Carefully invert the doughnuts onto a wire cooling rack and let cool completely, about 45 minutes.

5. Meanwhile, make the frosting: In a large bowl, using a hand or stand mixer, cream together the butter, vanilla, confectioners' sugar, milk, and food coloring on medium speed until smooth. Scoop the frosting into a piping bag fitted with a star tip.

6. Decorate the cooled doughnuts with the green frosting to look like boughs on a wreath. While the frosting is still wet, top it with the sprinkles. Serve immediately.

LITTLE HELPING HANDS (3+)

Let little helpers choose the sprinkles at the store. Then, let them finish the decorating of the doughnuts with the sprinkles they picked out.

KWANZAA WEEK

(DECEMBER 26–JANUARY 1)

Kwanzaa is a time for reflection, family, and community. It's a celebration of African American history and culture, and a commitment to positive values and social change. Kwanzaa is centered around seven principles, known as the Nguzo Saba:

- **UMOJA (UNITY).** Striving for and maintaining unity among the people.

- **KUJICHAGULIA (SELF-DETERMINATION).** Defining oneself, naming oneself, and creating for oneself.

- **UJIMA (COLLECTIVE WORK AND RESPONSIBILITY).** Building and maintaining our community together.

- **UJAMAA (COOPERATIVE ECONOMICS).** Building and maintaining our own stores, shops, and businesses.

- **NIA (PURPOSE).** Making our collective work and commitment to the liberation and transformation of our people our highest priority.

- **KUUMBA (CREATIVITY).** Doing always as much as we can, in the way we can, in order to leave our community more beautiful and beneficial than we inherited it.

- **IMANI (FAITH).** Believing in our people, our parents, our leaders, and the righteousness and victory of our struggle.

SWEET POTATO PIE

SERVES 8

Nonstick cooking spray

2 large sweet potatoes

1 cup (200 g) granulated sugar

½ cup (110 g) brown sugar

¼ cup (½ stick or 55 g) salted butter, melted

2 large eggs

1 teaspoon vanilla extract

½ teaspoon ground cinnamon

¼ teaspoon ground ginger

¼ teaspoon ground nutmeg

¼ teaspoon salt

1 refrigerated piecrust (9 inches, or 23 cm)

Whipped cream, for serving

1. Preheat the oven to 400°F (200°C). Grease a 9-inch (23 cm) pie plate with nonstick cooking spray.

2. Pierce the sweet potatoes several times with a fork, then place them in a baking dish. Bake for 45 to 60 minutes, until soft. Remove the potatoes from the oven and let cool enough to be handled. Remove and discard the skin, then add the flesh to a large bowl and mash it with a fork.

3. Add the granulated sugar, brown sugar, butter, eggs, vanilla, cinnamon, ginger, nutmeg, and salt and whisk until smooth.

4. Unroll the piecrust into the prepared pie plate and press it into the bottom and sides of the plate. Pour the filling into the crust.

5. Bake for 45 to 60 minutes, or until a toothpick inserted in the center comes out clean. Let the pie cool at room temperature for about 1 hour, then refrigerate for about 1 hour more before slicing and serving with whipped cream.

BIG KIDS IN THE KITCHEN (7+)

Ask your big kid if they would like to mash the potatoes for the pie. They can either use a fork, a potato masher, or a whisk to get the job done.

SWEET CORNBREAD

SERVES 12

Nonstick cooking spray
1 cup (125 g) all-purpose flour
1 cup (180 g) yellow cornmeal
1 cup (200 g) granulated sugar
3½ teaspoons baking powder
1 teaspoon salt
1 cup (240 ml) whole milk
⅓ cup (75 ml) vegetable oil
1 large egg

Serving Suggestions

Honey
Butter
Jam

1. Preheat the oven to 400°F (200°C). Grease a 9-inch (23 cm) pie plate with nonstick cooking spray.

2. In a large bowl, whisk together the flour, cornmeal, sugar, baking powder, and salt. Add the milk, oil, and egg and whisk until everything is wet. Pour the batter into the prepared pie plate.

3. Bake for 20 to 25 minutes, until a toothpick inserted in the center of the cornbread comes out clean.

4. Slice into wedges and serve warm or at room temperature with honey, butter, and/or jam.

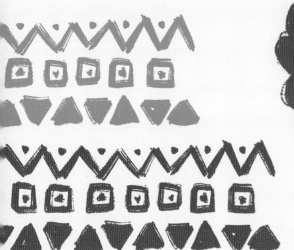

TWEENS ON THE SCENE (11+)

Whisking together ingredients is a breeze, and your tween can do it. Just help them measure all the ingredients, because a mis-measurement can lead to disaster.

COLLARD GREENS

SERVES 6

1 ham hock

1 tablespoon vegetable oil

1 cup (110 g) chopped yellow onion

1 tablespoon minced garlic

1 large bunch collard greens, washed, trimmed, and chopped

2 tablespoons apple cider vinegar

1 teaspoon paprika

½ teaspoon salt

½ teaspoon ground black pepper

3 cups (720 ml) chicken broth

1. Place the ham hock in a large pot, cover with water, and bring to a boil over medium heat. Reduce the heat to low and let simmer for 1 hour, or until the ham hock is tender. Transfer the ham hock to a cutting board and discard the water. Cut the ham hock into pieces.

2. In the same pot, add the oil, onion, and garlic over medium heat and cook, stirring occasionally, for about 5 minutes, or until the onion is softened. Sir in the collard greens, ham hock, vinegar, paprika, salt, and pepper.

3. Add the chicken broth, bring to a boil, then reduce the heat to low and let simmer for 1 hour, or until the greens are tender. Serve immediately.

BUDDING SOUS-CHEFS (17+)

This recipe is not complicated but it is mostly on the stovetop, so make sure you have a sous-chef who understands stove safety and to use hot pads when handling hot pots!

Index

Acknowledgments

Thank you to my best friend and favorite person in the whole wide world, Danny. I cannot put into words what you mean to me, but just know I love you.

The concept for the book started in 2019, when I made an online club for my kids and their friends to cook and eat the same foods the same weeks and lift each other up in trying new foods. My kids are not adventuresome eaters, so I thank Elliot, Hazel, and Clifford for stepping out of their comfort zones and at least tasting every single dish as part of the Club.

Thank you to my parents, Jeff and Karen Peterson, for feeding me a wide variety of dishes while growing up and encouraging my culinary curiosity. And thank you to them for continuing to be so supportive of my writing career.

Thank you to my agent, Joe Perry, for making this dream a reality, and for Erin Canning at The Quarto Group for welcoming me to the Rock Point family.

About the Author

Ashley Craft is the author of the best-selling *The Unofficial Disney Parks* cookbook series and *The Unofficial Universal Theme Parks Cookbook*. *Weeknight Wonders* is her seventh cookbook.

She loves to watch movies, eat out at restaurants, and travel with her family. She lives in Minnesota with her husband, Danny; their children, Elliot, Hazel, and Clifford; and their cats, Figgy, Strider, and Kelpie. Follow her on Instagram @UnofficialTasteTester.